THE DONUT THEORY

SOULY-4-YOU MINISTRY

THE DONUT THEORY

MEDITATIONS AND INSPIRATION FOR THE CHURCH OFFICE

LINDA GILLIS

WESTBOW
PRESS
A DIVISION OF THOMAS NELSON

The characters and events in this book are based on true incidents. In some
cases, names have been changed because of the sensitivity of the story.

All scripture quotations in this publication are from *The Message*.
Copyright © by Eugene H. Peterson 1993, 1994, 1995, 1996, 2000,
2001, 2002. Used by permission of NavPress Publishing Group.

WestBow Press books may be ordered through booksellers or by contacting:

WestBow Press
A Division of Thomas Nelson
1663 Liberty Drive
Bloomington, IN 47403
www.westbowpress.com
1-(866) 928-1240

ISBN: 978-1-4497-8127-9 (sc)
ISBN: 978-1-4497-8129-3 (hc)
ISBN: 978-1-4497-8128-6 (e)

Library of Congress Control Number: 2012924356

Printed in the United States of America

WestBow Press rev. date: 02/12/2013

To my mother, Olive Sampson,
who modeled for her children how a
strong work ethic and trust in God are
partners in faith. The best advice Mom
gave me is when times are tough,
"Think happy thoughts!"

And, to my husband Glen, our children,
Mike, Karen, and Susan, and
grandchildren, Mikaila, Nate, and
Mason, for their love and patience, and
for providing me with the best reason
to work less and play more.

Most of all, I thank God for making it
possible for me to recall the parables
for *The Donut Theory*.

I owe it all to little chocolate donuts.
—*John Belushi*

Table of Contents

Preface

The Donut Theory is more than a book about a fried and frosted round piece of dough with a hole in the middle. It's a book written to inspire and encourage those who serve God in the church office, who find that, like a donut, there are too many sides of serving God to bite off at one time, and sometimes "spiritual wholeness" is missing.

The comic strip, *Cathy* (the brainchild of Cathy Guiswite), gave me inspiration for the title *The Donut Theory*. Years ago, I cut out a *Cathy* comic strip from the newspaper and taped it to the wall above my computer. In the first frame, Cathy was at her desk, surrounded by a stack of work. In the last frame, she put on her coat, and the balloon above her head said, "I'm going for donuts."

Besides running for donuts during a stressful time in my office, many donuts were lifted to celebrate good times—a birthday or the birth of a grandchild. A box of donuts miraculously appeared each year at the completion of the annual report as a gratitude offering. For those who knew me well, a chocolate cake donut with a clear sugary glaze, made a great bribe or peace offering.

Every meditation in this book begins with a short scripture reference from the *The Message Bible*, the Bible written in everyday language. John 5:3 served as my guide for writing *The Donut Theory:* "If I were simply speaking on my own account, it [this book] would be an empty, self-serving witness."

I've concluded each story with a short prayer, punctuated with a comma instead of a period. Actor/comedian Gracie Allen was credited for saying, "Never place a period where God has placed a comma." I invite you to continue in prayer while reflecting on the message.

I encourage those who work in the church office to place this book close to his or her workstation, where it can be picked up (along with a cup of coffee or tea) and read for a quick meditation moment. Invite other staff members to join you for devotions. Perhaps you will learn a new trick for your trade, and chuckle about how this book will dispel the rumor that serving in the church office is such a *fun job* and such a *peaceful place* to hang out. A few of the stories may even bring tears—tears of the reality of the special ministry of serving in the church office.

Should you find some of the stories in this book to be a bit corny—it is something you might expect from an author who grew up on a farm in Iowa.

Blessed reading!

L.C.G.

Finding Peace and Joy

Do not forget all his benefits. Psalm 103:2

Jesus called his disciples to follow him. They didn't have a clue what they were getting into—like me when I got my first job in the church. Before my children were born, I worked for the social service agency in our county and had daily exposure to child neglect, seniors struggling to stay in their homes, and single moms trying to live on a welfare check. Years later, when the pastor of my church approached me about a part-time job, I figured working in the church would be a cakewalk compared with working in a public agency. *This might be a fun job and so peaceful!*

It didn't take long for the honeymoon to end, and I began to wonder if this *was* the job for me. There was never enough time to finish everything in my in-box and not everyone who called the office wanted to tell me what a great job I was doing. The joy of working for my pastor dissipated a bit when I found out he was as human as my own husband, and just as disorganized.

The first churches I served were single-pastor parishes. I loved the volunteers who religiously showed up and worked hard. I soon realized that the joy I found working in the church emanated from those who already had the peace I'd been seeking.

When serving in the large church, my workweek was full of challenges and surprises. On Friday evenings as I left my office, I'd stop and look at the neatly stacked pile of worship booklets ready for the ushers. It always gave me a sense of pride and relief! I'd leave the church with Peace, and on the drive home, Joy lifted my spirits. By Monday morning, I looked forward to going back to work and doing it all over again.

Lord, you make all things possible, over and over again,

Walking Carefree

Now I stroll at leisure with God in the sunlit fields of life. Psalm 57:13

When I moved to Arizona, I went to work at a retreat center called *Spirit in the Desert*. The name of the center captivated me, as did its mission statement: *To provide hospitality to those who come and rest for awhile in the desert.* The center sat on a little hill in a village, fittingly called Carefree.

No one hurries in Carefree. The streets are named to remind everyone to chill out, relax, and enjoy the village. There are no fast food or chain restaurants. Merchants button up their businesses before suppertime and tourists move on.

Each evening, as the blistering sun began to fade, I'd lace my walking shoes and head into the streets for a long walk to refresh my spirit. Companions were welcome, as long as they abided with the unspoken agreement to walk in silence—to listen to nature, perhaps a chorus of birds accompanied by a percussion of wind whipping through the hills.

I'd leave my office on Elbow Bend Road and amble down Nonchalant Avenue. If I passed another walker, I'd nod my head in greeting and continue circling around Easy Street and then saunter up Ho Hum Road. A quick veer to the right and I'd stroll on to Tranquil Trail for a few blocks. A short jog up East Carefree Drive and a quick left turn, Rocking Chair Lane invited me to stop. However, I'd continue on and float down Dream Street. A short block later, I'd pause on Serene Street and sit on a boulder to meditate and listen to the chants of coyotes reverberating between the mountains. I'd watch cottontails race around creosote bushes, while keeping a watchful eye for rattlesnakes, a band of javelina, or a scraggly gray coyote.

Before the path became illuminated by only stars and moonlight, I'd wander back to Spirit in the Desert in time to bid farewell to the sun as it slipped between layers of pink, purple, and orange taffeta clouds, before fading behind Black Mountain.

Dear Lord, thank you for restful places that renew my spirit,

Worry, Sorry, & Faith

He assigned a guardian angel to each of them. Deuteronomy 32:8

One day I received an e-mail forwarded from a friend who wrote, "You'll want to see this one!" Most often, I delete the dozens I get each week, but curiosity got the best of me, and I opened the attachment. Three animated angels flew in front of me, dancing to music that could have lulled me to sleep. Each angel had a name and a caption: *Worry* looks around; *Sorry* looks back; *Faith* looks up!

The message went on to say, "These three angels are sent to you, yada, yada, yada, send them on, etc., etc." *This is a keeper*, I thought, and forwarded it to three friends—one who worries about every little thing, one who obsesses over every decision, and another who is an example of how to live by faith.

During the day I imagined *Worry* shaking her head and finger at me as I fretted about how I'd be able to get two rooms set up for meetings, make coffee, and order lunch for the Synod Executive Committee while answering four telephone lines!

I pictured *Sorry* with her head bowed and hands folded, praying for me, "Help Linda figure out she doesn't have to play God."

I invited *Faith* to ride on my shoulders and massage the heaviness and stress with her heavenly hands.

I came to realize that when I trusted God, my own abilities, and other staff members to help me get through a busy day, I could give *Worry* and *Sorry* the day off.

Dear Lord, thank you for sending angels to
watch over us while we work—especially Faith,

The first Friday in June is "National Donut Day" in the USA. It was started by the Chicago Salvation Army in 1938 to celebrate Salvation Army lassies who volunteered their cooking skills in Europe.

Wishing Away Today

Don't worry about tomorrow. It will take care of itself.
You have enough to worry about today. Matthew 6:34

Some days are harder than others. I'd like to wish them away . . .
Tomorrow, tomorrow, I love you tomorrow, as Annie sang in the popular
musical by the same name. However, she always ended the song with
you're always a day away.

One Monday morning I arrived at the office—full of smiles,
humming a little tune I'd heard on the radio, ready to tackle the week.
I retrieved the messages from the answering machine and heard the
familiar gruff voice of a retired pastor. He sounded as if he had gotten
up on the wrong side of the bed, demanding a callback *immediately*! As
I dialed his number, my perky disposition began to wilt. By noon—in
between answering the phone and signing off on deliveries—I had
ripped paper out of every hiding place in the copy machine, reset the
locked-out postage meter, and found the server for one of my co-
workers whose computer said, "Can't find the server."

After a quick lunch, I sat down at my desk and sighed. The telephone
jolted me back into action. "Suck it up and just answer the phone," I
told myself. A calming voice greeted me, "Hello, Linda. This is Steve
[the bishop, who was also my boss]. How's your day going?" I forced a
smile into my voice, "It's going great," I said, trying to convince myself.
I transferred the call and took three deep breaths. My pulse returned
to normal, and the challenges of the morning seemed trivial.

I thanked God for the encouraging voice that quieted my soul and
helped to put a smile back on my face.

Creator God, help me find a way to start over on a bad day,
and to look for the good things happening around me,

When Not to Say No

*Summing it all up, friends, I'd say you'll do best by filling your
minds and meditating on things "true, noble, reputable . . .
the best, not the worst."* Philippians 4:8

"There will be no Sunday school next Sunday." As I read these words,
I wondered, *Why not?*

We live in a negative world with daily news of wars raging around
the world, and violence at home, work, and in our communities. The
word *no* finds its way into government agencies, classrooms, sports
events, and creeps into our churches.

When visiting different churches, I've seen negative signs lurking
inside and outside of the building: "No entrance," "No parking in
front of the church," or "No right turn." I've thought how "Enter at
next driveway," "Reserved for first-time visitors," or "Exit to your left"
would be more inviting.

Years ago I went to a seminar about communication in the
church and learned how *no* can have a negative impact when printed
in newsletters and bulletins. "No church school next Sunday" might
make the reader think the church does not take the children's ministry
program seriously. It is better to provide the answer in advance: "Church
school will be in recess next Sunday due to the special worship service
for families."

I've seen *no* shouted in announcements by being printed in **bold**
letters, emphasized with *italics*, <u>underscored</u>, and made larger than the
rest of the words. **_<u>NO!</u>_**

It is okay to use the word no in the church, such as in: "No, we
won't accept *no* for an answer!"

Lord, help us support your ministry in a positive way,

What's Your Task for Today?

Whatever your task, put yourselves into it. Colossians 3:23

The Church Parochial Report lay open on my desk with several empty columns staring back at me. Each year, I'd have to remind the staff members who still owed me numbers or figures that the report needed to be in the mail by April 1. When I finally stuffed the report into an envelope and dropped it in the mail, I'd rejoice. *Thank God! I don't have to do this for another year!*

There were times when I came back to work after a nice lunch, ready to continue working on the bulletin, and found a little yellow sticky note attached to a non-expected project saying, "I need this tomorrow. Thanks." My lunch stopped digesting and I had all I could do to refrain from running out of the building screaming like a mad woman.

Somehow, the projects always were completed in time. I learned through years of working under different administrations to build time into my schedule for emergency projects (like funeral service preparation) by using this formula: O + P = LS (Organization, Plus Prioritizing, Equals Less Stress). I also figured out that I'd never get an Academy Award for playing the role of Super Woman, and looked for a supporting actor to help me get through the scene.

In one of the offices in which I worked, we relied heavily on a volunteer who learned quickly and became skilled in so many ways that we eventually hired her to fill a part-time position. It was a match made in heaven and a boost to the support staff, knowing she was available to be called on to save the day.

If tasks in an office become *ministry impossible*, it may be time to speak to a supervisor or the pastor, instead of whining to co-workers. After all, competent and reliable administrative support is hard to replace!

Lord, help me remember I can only do so much in one day,

The Little Red Hen

*When he was alone with his disciples, he went over everything,
sorting out the tangles, untying the knots.* Mark 4:34

Late one Friday afternoon the deliveryman stacked a dozen cases of copy paper in the same hallway hundreds of little kids would be running past to get to their Sunday morning classrooms. I put out a call to the staff in the front office, "Who can help me put away the copy paper before we leave today?"

"Not I," said the receptionist. "I'm sorry, my husband and I have reservations for an early dinner."

"Not I," said the secretary. "I came in early and need to get home."

Just like in the book, *The Little Red Hen*, no one wanted to help me. *I'll shelve the paper by myself!* I thought. One by one, I cut through strapping tape, ripped off the lids, and shelved the paper until a rainbow of colors adorned the shelves—ready for the hens and roosters in the office to grab for their projects.

By 5:30, I'd deposited the last of the boxes into the recycling bin and called my husband to tell him I'd be late—again.

I don't mind working late now and then. When the rest of the staff goes home, the church becomes my quiet sanctuary—just me and God hanging out.

There are times when the Hen story had a different ending: "Hey, Linda," Ann said, "you've put in a long day. Go home. I'll run the inserts for the bulletin."

*Lord, in the office we learn to work as a team, just as Jesus and his disciples.
Thank you for the opportunity to serve you with my friends in Christ,*

Legend has it that dunking donuts became a trend when
actress Mae Murray accidentally dropped her donut
into a cup of coffee while dining at Lindy's Deli
on Broadway in New York City. (Source: www.donuss.com)

In His Image

Among us, you are all equal. Galatians 3:28

I dug deeply into my workbag for my car keys. It was 4:30 and I could finally go home. It had been one of those days when I left my house a few minutes late and ended up stalled in traffic behind two cars that had collided on Grand Avenue. The postage machine had run out of money, and the automatic download over the phone line wouldn't cough up the funds I requested. Before noon, I'd spilled tea on my new message pad. And, the phones—all four lines rang continuously, each caller needing something "right now" or didn't want to leave a message on voicemail.

As I headed for the door, the phone rang. I reached over the counter and picked up the receiver, forced a smile in my voice, and recited, "Synod Office, this is Linda. How may I help you?" A familiar voice spouted, "This is Walter. I need to talk with the bishop right away." I whispered a quick prayer for the bishop and transferred the call, guessing Walter didn't want to *talk with* anyone, but needed to download his frustrations. "And he thinks he's having a bad day," I muttered to myself.

On my way to the door, I paused and stared at a picture of Jesus, a farewell gift from the retreat center. The artist, William Zdinak, had painted the head and shoulder of Jesus by using faces of famous people, like Pope John XXIII, Ghandi, President Kennedy, and members of the artist's own family. He called the painting *In His Image*. When asked about the painting, he wrote, "We are 'all one in Christ,' as St. Paul has told us. Hurting one, we all hurt; helping one, we help all."

I tried to imagine Walter's face as part of the collage, and mine, too.

Dear Jesus, help me remember when I help others,
I become part of your image, too,

Stormy Days

He made the storm stop and the sea be quiet. Psalm 107:29

I grew up on a farm in Iowa. During tornado season, Mom watched the southwest skies for dark clouds churning up a storm. "I don't like the looks of those clouds," she'd announce and march my brothers and me down to the damp cellar to wait out the storm. I'd hover on the step above the dirt floor, with my arms wrapped tightly around my knees, and listen to branches of the elm tree slap against the tin roof of the coal shed outside the cellar door. Mother, holding the kerosene lantern, watched for a streak of sunlight to appear under the cellar door. When she'd declare, "Storm's over!" I'd bolt out of the cellar like a chicken fleeing the coop. The cellar was far scarier than any storm.

I've created a few internal storms during my workdays. One time I was in such a hurry to get to an appointment, I ran 500 copies upside down on the backside of a bulletin. I mentally kicked myself around the office the rest of the day for wasting paper, copier ink, and my time.

The all-time worst punishment I inflicted on myself happened when I failed to review the agreement on a copy machine before the lease expired. I missed the ninety-day notice needed to opt-out of the lease. No matter how much I argued with the leaseholder, the office was stuck with another year of payments on the worthless machine. That storm seemed like a weeklong low-pressure system stalled out in my head.

Just like Mom who took me to the cellar to wait out a storm, God guided me through a stormy day in the office with an extra dose of grace and an understanding, forgiving boss who said, "Linda, stop beating yourself up! Everyone makes mistakes."

Dear Lord, help me remember that human error and
self-worth are not related to one another.

Time to Play

*It's in Christ that we find out who we are and what
we are living for.* Ephesians 1:11

When I'm passionate about what I'm doing, California could slide into
the Pacific Ocean, and I wouldn't know it until I hit the Save button
on my computer and turned on the TV. My days fly by when I'm doing
a project in the office that uses my creative juices—like organizing a
supply cabinet or rearranging the tract rack.

I worked to financially help put my children through college, to
buy groceries, and to make a car payment. However, I discovered *work
and pay, with no play*, makes for long days.

Years ago, one of our civic organizations staged a fundraiser by
capturing employees and putting them into a jail cell until they raised
bail. One of our pastors had turned in Sally, our church administrator,
to the "authorities." Two of Naperville's finest police officers came
to the office, snapped handcuffs on her wrists, and stuffed her into
a squad car. All afternoon, the rest of the staff snickered about how
Sally had been set up.

On the way out the door, Sally had wisely stuffed her Rolodex into
her bag and easily made bail (with the help of the generous donations
she requested of the staff).

Co-workers can't be sent to jail just for the fun of it, but can look
for opportunities to perk up the workplace. One spring a half dozen
of us in the office forfeited our lunch breaks to learn to tap dance.
We learned a special routine to perform at a farewell program for a
pastor who'd been taking tap-dancing lessons. I wasn't very good with
the shuffle-ball-change stuff, but it was worth a lot of laughs, and a
standing ovation by Pastor Al.

Dear God, bless our work and our play,

Don't Just Change Your Dress

Change your life, not just your clothes. Joel 2:13

Every Monday morning as I got ready for work, I would put on the same clothes I'd worn to church Sunday morning. It made it easy—I didn't have to think about what to wear, and I started the week looking my Sunday best.

Several years ago, I spent three months working at a law office as a temporary employee. I had lost a lot of weight after surgery and had inherited a whole wardrobe from someone who had shrunk out of her clothes. Every day, I put on a different combination of skirts, blouses, or sweaters, and never wore the same outfit twice. It became a game to me. I was sure no one noticed my extensive wardrobe.

Years later, I ran into Monica (my former supervisor from that law firm) at a luncheon for businesswomen. She looked at me and at the dress I was wearing, and said, "I remember you. You're the one who wore a different outfit every day for three months!" I blushed to think how shallow I must have appeared to everyone in that office.

They didn't know I'd just quit a job at another law firm that had taken over my life—physically and emotionally—and how I'd gotten my new wardrobe.

Before I left the luncheon I thanked Monica for the three months the law office had given me, as a temporary employee, to heal—and to change career paths back to the church office.

*Dear God, thank you for giving me signs of when
I need to change my life—not just my clothes,*

According to the Guinness Book of World Records, the record for most donuts eaten at one sitting is held by Eric "Badlands" Booker, who ate 49 glazed donuts in eight minutes.

Holy Week?

When trouble and distress surround you like a whirlwind,
I will laugh and make fun. Proverbs 1:27

A few years ago at a retreat, everyone was given a big campaign-style button with white puffy clouds floating on a deep indigo sky and a tall white cross in the center. Around the rim are the words: TOO BLESSED . . . TO BE STRESSED. I keep mine pinned to a bulletin board next to my desk.

For many years, I served in a congregation with over 4,000 members and five worship services. I produced what seemed like millions of worship booklets, all twelve to sixteen pages long. I started right after lunch on Tuesday and delivered the final copies to the copy room by noon on Thursday. Occasionally the director of music or pastor made a last-minute change to the service, and I'd automatically shift into high-stress mode. The palms of my hands dripped perspiration onto the keyboard, and my fingers hit the wrong keys. Sometimes I'd screw up a page alignment and have to print the whole bulletin again and transfer the pasted-up music before skidding into the copy room a few minutes after noon.

It only took one season working during Lent to realize there wasn't much sacred about that week between Palm Sunday and Easter called Holy Week. With all the extra services, and a bumper crop of bulletins needed for Easter Sunday, I relied heavily on my proofreaders. One volunteer, with an eagle eye, became a saint when she caught a potential bulletin blooper that referred to a woman on the church council as the *Palm* Reader, instead of Psalm Reader for the Maundy Thursday service.

It takes more than a lapel button to transform me from being a well-seasoned stressor to a tamed tiger in the office. I learned that in order to stay well below the stress radar level, I needed to start Holy Week preparation soon after Ash Wednesday and to stock up on my favorite tea, "Tension Tamer."

Dear God, help me find one way to reduce my stress today,

Proofreaders in the Pew

Kind mercy wins over harsh judgment every time.
James 2:13

One would think every bulletin printed would be bound and filed in the Library of Congress, instead of being circulated into the recycling bin on the way out of the sanctuary. Mistakes happen! I occasionally read typos in a book and regularly see notifications of corrections in my local newspaper. Proofreaders miss stuff. Almost anything is forgivable, *except* names. Turn *Byron* into *Bryon* and a new name has been created for the name-your-baby books. Change *Katharine* into *Katherine* and the woman is no longer Irish.

I appreciate being corrected for errors and omissions, but not during worship when someone sitting next to me nudges me in the ribs to point out an error. Or, how about finding a bulletin spread out on your desk first thing Monday morning with words circled and underlined! That's not the way I like to start my week. Therefore, I've created a form for pew proofreaders:

Pew Proofreader's Pad

To: _____ Re: _____

For your information, _____ is spelled _____.

The correct date for the _____ meeting is _____.

One good thing I liked about the 99% error-free bulletin:

_____

I am available to proof the bulletin each Thursday morning.

Signed: _____ Dated: _____

Please deliver this form to the church office, along with a
Butterfinger or Snickers candy bar (or a *Hershey's Kiss*). Thanks!

Dear Jesus, help me accept my errors with grace,

Ability or Motivation

But when Jesus turned and saw the disciples, he corrected Peter.
He said to him, "Satan, get away from me! You are thinking
like everyone else and not like God." Mark 8:33

"Ability is what you are capable of doing.
Motivation determines what you do.
Attitude determines how well you do it." (Lou Holtz)

My first job out of high school was with the State of Iowa Social Service Agency. I'd had no experience working with a Dictaphone, but was sure I could learn to drive the tape machine with my foot and type at the same time. For eight hours a day, I transcribed case reviews for social workers and typed words I'd never heard of before, like *arteriosclerosis*. As faithfully as the sun rose, a tall stack of files greeted me every morning. No matter how fast I typed, I never got to the bottom of the stack. I tackled each file with the attitude: *Just get it done!*

I'd been on the job about a month and thought I was doing a good job, until my boss called me into his office. He suggested I work a little slower and look up words in the dictionary if I wasn't sure how they were spelled. (This was long before computers and my coveted spell checker.) After I got over the shock that I didn't spell as well as I thought I did, I became a better employee and enjoyed learning new words.

Confronting employees about their errors, weaknesses, or out-of-control attitudes is tough, but necessary, in order to keep the office running smoothly. Jesus was a great supervisor and trained his disciples how to work with people. He challenged them in their thinking—especially Peter, whom Jesus called on the carpet for an attitude adjustment a few times, too.

Dear Jesus, thank you for caring and for grace-filled
supervisors in the church office,

Blowouts!

Be kind to me, God, I've been kicked around long enough.
Psalm 9:13

When I was a kid on the farm, my family took a week off from chores in the summer and went camping. On our first trip, Dad borrowed a military-style tent with no floor. Mom stuffed frayed quilts and old bed pillows into feed sacks and filled a beer cooler with produce from the garden and meat from the freezer. Dad climbed up on the sideboards of the car and stacked the camping gear into a cartop carrier he'd constructed out of two-by-fours and plywood. Then he covered it with a stiff green tarp and tied it down with baling twine. Everything else went into the trunk. As I think back on those days, we must have resembled a band of gypsies.

My three brothers and I piled into the rusty Chevy, along with Mom and Dad, and we headed to Clear Lake, about ninety miles north of our farm. About forty-five miles into the trip, Dad shoved the gearshift into low, and the car thumped to the side of the road. "Flat tire," he growled. Dad changed the tire, and then he sat all alone by the side of the road, adding another patch to the old inner tube. After he stuffed it back into the tire, he used a hand pump to inflate the tube to make the new spare tire, which we needed before we got to the lake!

I've had a few *flat tires as I've worked*—like the Friday afternoon when I had one more job to copy and the machine stubbornly displayed: **CALL FOR SERVICE**. I stared at the bulletin that the wedding coordinator would be looking for in a couple of hours. *Now what?* I thought. Then I remembered that a secretary from the church down the street had used our copier when their machine had broken down on a Friday afternoon. I called their office and within an hour the bulletins were copied, neatly folded, and ready for the rehearsal.

Lord, send the Holy Spirit to keep our spirits inflated,

Centennial Beach

*If any of you has a hundred sheep, and one of them
gets lost, what will you do?* Luke 5:4

During my stay-at-home mom days, I'd pack up my kids during the
summer and head to Centennial Beach for an afternoon. Thousands
of people, mostly pre-teens and little children, came to the pool every
day. Lifeguards were perched all around the beach, and signs reminded
parents: WATCH YOUR CHILDREN!

The beach was a rock quarry before being converted to a public
swimming pool. Tons of sand led up to the pool's edge, where moms
gathered to chat and watch their toddlers waddle around in ankle-deep
water. A gradual downward slope to the lap lanes gave swimmers of all
sizes a great place to play. No swimmer could venture into the 30-foot
deep end of the pool without proving they could swim the length of
the pool. Overall, it was a fun, safe place to spend the summer.

About once a week, an announcement came over the loud speaker:
"Clear the pool. Everyone out!" A child was lost. Lifeguards sprang off
their towers and strapped on SCUBA gear. Adult swimmers formed
a human chain across the width of the pool and searched with their
feet while walking toward the deep end. When I had someone to
watch my kids, I'd join in, praying that no one would stumble across
a child. Fortunately, the child was always found in the bathhouse or
wandering around the playground. No matter how many human chains
were formed during the summer, the adults and children took the
announcement seriously.

I am comforted to know that God moves into action the moment
I put out a panicky request—no matter how often or how close I am
to drowning in my own problems or the load of work gathered on my
desk.

*Thank you, God, for the shepherds in my life who model
how you care for all your children,*

Attitude

Bridle your anger, trash your wrath, cool your pipes—
it only makes things worse. Psalm 37:8

When I worked for the synod of our church, I drove twenty-two miles on congested surface streets to get to my office. After a year of this commute, I found myself turning into a witch on wheels! By the time I got to work, I'd hand-signaled crazed drivers, cut through a few parking lots to avoid another stoplight, and eaten half my lunch.

To amuse myself into thinking I really enjoyed the time I spent in my Toyota, I listened to the radio—NPR or *Air America*. However, starting my workday with the casualty report from the war in Iraq, or hearing the Democrats and Republicans verbally slug it out over immigration or the budget, was enough to ruin my breakfast and my drive. I borrowed books-on-tape from the library, but the drone of the reader's voice had about the same effect as Sominex.

One day I slammed hard on the brakes to avoid hitting a stray dog, and my workbag tumbled off the seat, spilling everything onto the floor mat. At the next light, I picked up the current edition of *Guideposts* magazine that I'd planned to read during my lunch break. I began to read an article about a woman who was tossed out of her canoe into the raging rapids of the Colorado River. *How did she survive?* I wondered, and as the light turned to green, I dropped the magazine onto my lap. At the next red light, I read a few paragraphs and hated to put the magazine down. By the time I got to work, I'd sat through enough red lights to finish the story.

My attitude about the commute changed that day. I kept small items on my lap and even began to look forward to the long red traffic lights. [Please note: I *did not* read and drive at the same time, even when tempted!]

Thank you, God, for giving me opportunities to find ways to
improve my attitude on the way to work,

G.P.S.

*Now get yourselves ready. I'm sending my Angel ahead of
you to guard you in your travels.* Exodus 23:20

My husband and I have a new traveling companion—Mr. Know-It-All,
a Global Positioning System. "Why do you need that thing?" I asked,
with a whine I reserve to show disapproval. I've navigated us across
the USA on many occasions (and brag about my 98 percent accuracy,
with no more than three turnarounds per trip). Now, everywhere we
go "Mr. KIA" speaks in a monotone baritone voice while a green snake
wiggles its way across the display screen.

My feelings are hurt. Perhaps I'm a bit jealous that I've been
replaced by an obnoxious chatterbox plugged into the cigarette lighter.
Every time I hear "recalculating route" or "turn right in ten seconds,"
it's like a fork tine scraping over a china plate. It frequently interrupts
a book-on-tape just as the plot thickens. I'm all for working smarter,
not harder, but Mr. Know-It-All is a *byte* away from being removed of
his duties.

I felt the same way after I'd given notice to my supervisor that I'd
be retiring and was replaced by someone from the support staff. She
had observed my work for years and had been around the block in
other church offices. She didn't need a GPS to give her directions on
how to do the job.

As my duties were removed a little at a time, I began to feel like a
starting pitcher who was put on the bench to be used only as a closer.
However, on my last day of work, I left my office feeling as if I'd pitched
a no-hitter—confident that the office was in good hands.

*Lord, lead us every day through the paths it takes to
do the mission of the church,*

Lonely or Alone

I am lonely and troubled. Show that you care. Psalm 25:16

I dropped my toddler off at a friend's house every Friday morning so I could do the bulletins for the Sunday service in my small church in Beatrice, Nebraska. The job got me out of the house once a week, and I liked the spending money, but it was a *lonely* job. The pastor moved out of his office on that day and worked in the parsonage next door so that I could use the only typewriter in the building. The telephone rarely rang.

I would put a Gestetner master into the old Remington electric typewriter and cautiously type the service, trying not to make too many errors. The blue correction gunk was a mess to apply and hard to type over. Then I'd pray as I headed for the old mimeograph machine in the basement, "Please, God, don't let the machine gobble up my master." I'd sigh with relief when the meter registered 120 copies.

I'd hand-fold the bulletins and take them to the table in the narthex for the ushers to pick up on Sunday morning. On the way back to my office, I'd take a tour of the pews, tidy up the hymnals, remove crayon-artwork from the offering envelope holders, and occasionally dive under a pew to collect a Cheerio that had escaped the dust mop.

Years later, I worked for a large church and sometimes felt *alone*. My office was tucked away down the hall from the rest of the support staff. When I'd get the feeling of being all alone in the church, I'd take a break and stroll up and down the hallways looking for someone to chat with for a while—another staff member or someone stopping by to get their blood pressure checked by the parish nurse. In a few minutes, I'd be refreshed and ready to tackle my projects again.

Dear God, may I always feel your presence in my life,

M&Ms

*Lord, doesn't it bother you that my sister has left me
to do all the work by myself? Luke 10:40*

Jane served as the receptionist and membership secretary in our office. She'd slip behind her desk a few minutes before the office opened, could grab the phone receiver while pulling off her coat and tell the caller what time the Welcome Committee would be meeting, without looking at the calendar. I never needed to water the ivy on my desk, make coffee, or remind her to get ushers lined up for a funeral. At the end of the day, she'd put on her coat and shuffle toward the door yawning and muttering, "I'm pooped." Her middle name must have been *Martha*.

Amy helped Jane with the phones and assisted anyone who needed an extra pair of hands. She'd chat with a mother whose child was at choir rehearsal, linger after staff meetings until everyone went back to their office, and as she passed by Jane's desk, would flash her Shirley Temple smile and recite, "Sorry, Jane, I hope the phones weren't ringing off the desk." I wanted to ask her if her middle name was *Mary*.

A model assistant would be what I call an M&M—a combination of the biblical sisters Mary and Martha, one who shows up on time eager to serve, but knows when to shift into neutral and sit at the knee of someone who needs to talk. An M&M would look for opportunities to make a difference in how well the office runs for everyone.

Some days I'm a Mary; other days a Martha. My goal is to be an M&M.

Dear Lord, let us learn to be a little of Mary and Martha,

Rhode Islanders love their donuts. The density of donut shops is so thick that there is one shop for every 4,700 residents in the state.

The Lost Keys

Celebrate with me! I've found my lost sheep [keys]! Luke 15:6

I had borrowed the janitor's truck keys. A few minutes later when I went to put the keychain back in his cubby, I couldn't find them. I scratched my head, *Where are the keys? They were in my hands only a minute ago!*

I checked my pockets, got down on my knees and looked beneath my desk. I dashed out the door and retraced my steps—twice. No keys. As I passed by the volunteer desk where Joyce sat, she heard me mumbling about how I had lost the keys. "Linda," she said, "go, sit down, and get back to work! Ask God to help you find the keys. Tell him you're getting old and forgetful and need help."

I couldn't argue with her about getting old and forgetful. I slumped down in front of the monitor and heard Joyce say, "Now, work for a while and then get up and look for the keys." A few minutes later Joyce added, "Now go out and retrace your steps exactly where you walked when you lost the keys." I followed her instructions, and with each step I prayed, "Okay, God. Joyce said you'd help me find the keys, so where are they?"

I shuffled back to the entrance and opened the door for a member coming out. Deb noticed the puzzled look on my face. "What's up, Linda?" she asked. "I've lost some keys—I've searched everywhere and can't find them." Deb said she'd keep an eye open for them. I thanked her and went back to my office, slinking past Joyce, hoping she wouldn't tell me to sit down and pray again. That hadn't worked.

I'd been at my computer about five minutes when Deb jingled the key chain behind my back. "I found them in a handicapped space in the parking lot!" I grabbed her, gave her a big hug, and said, "Joyce didn't tell me God might assign the project to one of his servants!"

Dear God, thank you for angels who help me every day,

The Snake

But ask the animals what they think—let them teach you. Job 12:7

One day a woman came to my office at the retreat center and said, "There's a snake—a big one stretched out by the door to the chapel." I'd seen a few snakes that intimidated me enough to call the maintenance man. He'd take a long pole with pincers on the end and pick up the snake, drop it into a bucket, and move it far away from the buildings. But it was his day off!

I mustered up enough composure to follow the woman out the door, stop, and pick up the pole and bucket from the maintenance shed. I headed for the chapel praying, "God, help me get through this first-time confrontation with a snake so the guests can continue their retreat without the uninvited reptile!"

A crowd had gathered around the lounging snake, as if they were keeping it in a corral until I arrived. I sighed in relief when I recognized the distinct markings of a bull snake, instead of a rattlesnake I'd seen before.

With the pole and bucket, I looked official to the group, but my heartbeat and sweaty palms made me aware I was embarking on another *first* in my career working in the church. Just as I directed the pole to grab the snake at its midsection, a young man standing close by swooped down and picked up the snoozing creature. The startled snake whipped its head around and struck the guy on his arm. Everyone stepped back. I muffled my gasp. "I'm okay," he said. "This snake's bite won't hurt anyone."

I thanked the man (and God) all the way to the boulders behind the chapel where the snake was safely deposited away from the guests. I did feel sort of proud of myself for at least trying to be a brave snake remover.

Lord, thank you for watching out for me,

A Friendly Workplace

Try to live at peace with everyone! Live a clean life.
Hebrews 12:14

Tim McGuire writes a syndicated newspaper column *More than Work*. One week he wrote about the friendly workplace and how an organized workspace enhances production and becomes a point of pride for the employees. Mr. McGuire observed that workers in an organized workspace feel a sense of belonging.

I surveyed my office space—the reception area. Magazines overflowed on the small table between two guest chairs. Outdated brochures took up space on a shelf. A too-tall stack of fliers made it look as if no one was interested in the event. I tucked half the fliers into a cabinet and tossed the outdated material into the recycling bin. Fondly, I looked at four pictures of my granddaughter and removed three. I couldn't part with the one of her in her T-ball uniform.

I strolled through the rest of the suite, observed three boxes of paper leaning against the copy machine, and took two to the storage room. The bulletin board in the break room hosted an article posted six months earlier about how not to overeat during the Christmas season. I tossed it into the garbage can and re-arranged the posters announcing staff meetings and official holidays. Next, I opened storage cabinet doors and moved the most frequently used items to the front of the shelves. By the end of the day, pencils, pens, and markers were bunched in clear plastic bins with a label on the end.

I don't know if the rest of the staff felt a sudden sense of belonging, but the next time I needed a two-square-inch yellow sticky notepad, I put my fingers on it without ransacking the whole cupboard.

Dear Lord, increase in me an awareness of
how my space affects my guests and me,

I'll Rest Later

My chosen ones will have satisfaction in their work. They won't
work and have nothing come of it. Isaiah 65:22,23

Crabby! That's how I get when I don't get enough rest. Just ask my
husband.

Every spring the support staff at the synod office spends months
preparing for the annual assembly. Before going paperless, it took
the staff and volunteers several weeks to copy, collate, and insert the
reports into binders. We would shut down the duplicating machine
just in time to pack the van with boxes full of office supplies, worship
bulletins, and the extra three-ring binders for those who forgot their
own.

Every year we arrived a day before the pastors and lay delegates,
set up the temporary office, and helped vendors find their space in
the exhibit hall. That evening, we'd celebrate by having a nice dinner
together, and then everyone headed to his or her hotel rooms to get
a good night's sleep before the assembly action started first thing the
next morning.

During the next three days, we hung out in the makeshift office
to run off a missing report, replace nametags, direct traffic to meeting
rooms, or anything else to help the assembly run smoothly. By day
three, I found it difficult to muster up even a fake smile. "Can't they
bring their own dry markers?" . . . "Couldn't she have given us her
handouts to copy yesterday?" It was easy to forget that those who
had responsibilities for workshops or programs had to squeeze their
presentation planning into their normal busy schedule.

After returning home from the assembly, I'd take little catnaps
for a few days—not just because of the long days and tasks expected
of the support staff and volunteers, but also from the excitement of
being part of a large body of Christ, working to fulfill the mission of
the church.

Lord, thank you for the opportunity to serve,

Gifts of the Spirit

He brings gifts into our lives, much the same way that fruit appears in an orchard—things like affection for others, exuberance about life, serenity. Galatians 5:22

I'm thinking of words that begin with the letter *C* that either cause chaos or contentment in a Christ-centered, cozy church office:

Rude C's:

- **Cell phone ring tones**: I could tell how many times Julie's husband and each of her three kids called every day by the clever little ditties designated for each caller. It took all I could do to keep from telling Julie to keep her phone in her lunch bag in the refrigerator. (The girls in my former office are probably still telling about the day they heard my lunch bag ringing in the refrigerator.)
- **Chomping chewing gum:** I don't chew gum because when I look at someone who does, it's so distracting I miss half of what's being said. (I'd hate to have that happen when I'm talking.)
- **Careless disposal of banana peels:** This is huge. Throwing a banana peel in the office garbage can should be grounds for time off without pay. (Especially the ones ready to be mashed for banana bread.)

Good C's:

- **Cooperation:** Put the phone on vibrate and watch it dance across the desk.
- **Consideration**: Remove the chewing gum or nod your head and use sign language to communicate.
- **Courtesy:** Tightly secure banana peels in a plastic bag and throw the bag into the Dumpster outside the church, *or* better yet, just bring the banana bread.

Lord, help me to remember my P's, Q's, and C's,

Smile!

He puts a smile on my face. He's my God. Psalm 42:11

"Happiness is only a grin deeper than a frown." (Unknown)

I was deep into proofreading the worship booklet when a friend stopped by and asked, "What are you frowning about?" I didn't know I was frowning. "I guess it's just my way of concentrating," I replied. When she left, I thought about how much better it would be if I'd smile through my tasks. I considered putting a little mirror on my desk to remind me to smile but waved that thought away as I strongly dislike looking at myself in a mirror.

Some days in the church office, one has to look for things to smile about. I had a week like that when I broke every machine I touched. The network went down, then the power supply on my computer fried, the spare computer I was using gave me the dreaded "not responding" message, and I lost the draft of the bulletin I'd spent two hours typing. Besides that, I went home to an unmade bed, dishes in the sink, furniture still in the middle of the room (after my husband vacuumed), rugs in a heap on the patio waiting to be shaken, and garbage that didn't make it to the garbage can.

Some times co-workers forget to bring a smile to work. They need to be reminded that it takes 43 muscles to frown and only 17 to smile. Actually, I recently learned that it takes 11 muscles to frown and 12 to smile. So, it looks as if a smile *really* is a grin deeper than a frown, but worth the extra work.

Lots of things put a smile on my face—the joy of knowing the Lord, working with others who love the Lord, or the little surprises that interrupt my day in a good way, like when a member of the church brings in a box of donuts to say thanks to the staff for all we do around the church.

*Dear Lord, you are the mirror that reflects
joy and puts a smile in my heart,*

The Weakest Link

Honor God by accepting each other, as Christ
has accepted you. Romans 3:21

I inherited Darla, a part-time secretary, when I took the job as an office manager for a church office. She and her husband had been long-standing, vital members of the congregation. Everyone loved Darla for her warm heart and witty personality, but she marched to the tune of her constantly ringing cell phone.

First thing every morning, Darla made the rounds to greet everyone on her way to get a cup of coffee. When she sat down to work, she worked diligently. But if I gave her a project with a deadline, she'd get a migraine headache. I learned to give her projects that lived on forever, like posting the attendance or updating member records. In my mind, I saw Darla as the *weakest link* on our staff. There were days I wished she would stay home!

At home, Darla struggled with a rebellious teenager and a workaholic husband. One day, she told me that she always felt better at work than at home. At that moment, I knew Darla needed this job—not for the money, but to stay balanced. If I wanted to keep my sanity, I could either quit my job or adjust to Darla. The choice was simple: I needed my job to pay college tuition for my daughter; unlike Darla, who took her earnings to the mall.

I began to pray, "Dear God, help me get through the day without complaining about Darla." I started thanking God, and Darla, whenever she did something to make my work easier (even as simple as giving me the worship attendance figure by Monday noon instead of Wednesday). I learned to love her for who she is, and for every little way she served the Lord.

Lord, thank you for using Darla to teach me that serving
you and others begins at my desk,

If Not You, Who?

Tune your ears to the world of Wisdom;
set your heart on a life of Understanding. Proverbs 2:1

One corner of the copy room in the church had a counter with a sink, coffee machine, and a microwave. The staff, including the pastors, took turns making coffee and eating their share of cookies and pastries left behind from meetings. By Friday afternoon, the coffee cups stacked in the sink resembled a high-rise building ready to collapse.

Someone must have gotten tired of looking at the mess in the corner and put up a large sign over the sink: **IF NOT YOU, WHO? IF NOT NOW, WHEN?** I loved the sign and had high hopes it would bring awareness to everyone that we didn't have a self-cleaning coffee area.

Nothing changed. Perhaps the problem was that no one identified themselves as the *who* or the time as *now*. Whenever I couldn't stand the mess any longer, I'd fill the sink with hot sudsy water and wash the dishes, throw away the rock-hard coffeecake, and wipe tomato sauce from the inside of the microwave, while grumbling, "I work with a bunch of thoughtless pigs." (One of the pastors who previewed this book thought *he* was the one who washed all the coffee mugs!)

Perhaps our busy staff needed a more proactive approach to the mess in the kitchen—a sign-up sheet to pick a time to do the end-of-the week cleaning detail or to start a fund to hire a cleaning service.

Lord, if we don't talk about expectations, it's
possible no one really cares if the sink and
microwave are spotless. Thanks for the insight,

The size of the average donut hole is 4/5" in diameter.

Asleep at the Keyboard

He got up from prayer, went back to the disciples and found them asleep, drugged by grief. Luke 22:45

Top Five Excuses if Caught Sleeping at Your Desk
(Source Unknown)

No. 5: They told me at the blood bank this might happen.

No. 4: This is just a fifteen-minute power nap they raved about at the management course you sent me to.

No. 3: Whew! Guess I left the top off the Witeout®. You probably got here just in time.

No. 2: Did you ever notice sounds coming out of these keyboards when you put your ear down real close?

And, the **No. 1** best thing to say if you get caught sleeping at your desk: Raise your head slowly and say, ". . . In Jesus' name. Amen."

I looked up at my monitor and found kkkkk across the screen. *How long had I been dozing?* I wondered. I'd been a bit more tired at work than usual, but I'd never fallen asleep in my office. I mentioned my page of k's to a co-worker who suggested maybe I was trying to be Super Woman and to cut back on activities.

That night I looked at my appointment book. *How many things could I get out of next week?* I asked myself. "My circle meeting? Choir rehearsal? The parent/teacher conference for my daughter?" The week looked daunting. "Maybe I need to start taking vitamins," I told myself as I dropped the calendar back on the shelf.

The next time I nodded off. I called the choir director and said, "I need to take time off from the choir for a while."

Lord, please help me make the right choices for my days,

The Best and the Weakest

*The disciples came up and asked, [Jesus], "Why do you
tell stories?" I tell stories to create readiness, to nudge the
people toward receptive insight.* Matthew 13:10,14

I've always thought one's best quality can also be their weakest. I've
been told I have the gift for communicating—written and verbal. One
day my husband stopped in the office to take me home from work and
listened as I conversed with another secretary. On the way home he
said, "Sometimes you talk too much and don't give the other person a
chance to say what's on their mind."

After I decided to cook dinner for him, in spite of his frank
comment, I realized he was right. Sometimes when I get excited, I get
a bad case of motor mouth. The lips start the action, and the tongue
doesn't stop until it runs out of fuel. Usually, the subject matter is dear
to my heart—or a thorn in my side.

A new employee I once trained left the office at the end of the
first day with a blank look on her face that suggested, "Enough!" My
enthusiasm for working in the church had set my mouth going. I tried
to show her everything I knew and tell her how much she would love
working in the church office. After such verbal overload, I'm surprised
she came back the next day.

I've learned I can't tell someone in a day, or week, how to do a job
I've done for many years. One needs to work in the church at least a
year to figure out the rhythms—the swells and ebbing—of the tides
of the programs and projects. It's better to do the training as Jesus did
with his disciples—walk with them, listen to their needs, teach them
through stories, and pray for them.

*Lord, help us to train others with the grace and
respect Jesus showed in his ministry,*

No Dinner Tonight

I was a stranger and you welcomed me. Matthew 25:35

I looked at the clock in my office and quickly stuffed the bulletin material I was working on into a drawer, picked up my bag, and headed out the door. My daughter, Susan, had a pre-game color guard rehearsal in two hours. If I hurried, I would have just enough time to get home and cook a good meal for her before driving her to the high school. However, first I needed to make a quick stop at the grocery store for lettuce, pasta sauce, and milk.

I dashed into the store, grabbed a cart, and went directly to the produce department. While I squeezed a few heads of lettuce, an elderly man sauntered over and stood close to my cart. In a voice a little louder than a whisper, he said to me, "My son's coming to visit." I threw a head of lettuce into my cart and said, "That's nice. Have a good visit," and turned my cart toward the dairy cooler.

I picked up a gallon of milk, and out of the corner of my eye saw the same old guy shuffling over. Before I could escape, he said, "He hasn't been home for five years." I gave him an affirming nod and wheeled toward the checkout counter, grabbing the first bottle of pasta sauce I saw. *We could use some sodas for after the game,* I thought, and detoured to the side aisle. I leaned over to pick up a 12-pack of cola and heard the same voice. "He hasn't been home since his mother died."

"Lord, help me!" I silently prayed. "I gave myself five minutes to get in and out of this store, and this guy wants to tell me his life story!" At that moment, the anxiety in his eyes tugged at my heart. I wiped a stray strand of hair away from my eyes, leaned on the handle of my cart, and listened. I heard the story of a father and son so overcome with grief that they had said ugly things to one another. Then he asked, "What shall I say to him?" I looked into his worried eyes and placed my hand on his. "Just put your arms around him and give him a hug. The words will come."

Dear God, thanks for placing people in my life who need more than a nutritious meal, and for the concession stand at the football field,

Tackle the Gloomies

*Keep your eyes open, your lamp burning, so you don't
get musty and murky.* Luke 11:36

Misery loves company. Like it or not, we are influenced by people who have the cup half-empty syndrome. Sometimes situations give us a temporary down day. When Jesus was in deep sorrow in the Garden of Gethsemane, he called upon his disciples to stay with him, and they fell asleep!

As I get ready for work, I listen to the radio for the traffic and weather report. It frustrates me when I hear, "Today's going to be a *gloomy* day in the Valley." I'd be content to hear just the facts, "There's a possibility of rain today." Let me decide for myself if it's going to be a gloomy day.

Some people are caught up in the gloomy forecast and bring it to work. The following suggestions may help you combat gloomy days in the office:

- Wear a bright Hawaiian floral muumuu and a fake lei on a winter day. (Bring a sweater if you live in Minnesota.)
- Get a fake tattoo of a butterfly or hummingbird. (Put it where everyone can see it and so they will wonder if it's real.)
- Do acts of kindness, such as sharpening everyone's pencils. (Pop make-believe gloom balloons hovering overhead.)

If all fails, bake your favorite chocolate chip cookies and take them to work while they are still warm. No one can stay in a gloomy mood after taking a bite of a homemade cookie.

Lord, help me be patient with myself during gloomy days,

Who Will Go?

Whom shall I send? Who will go for us?
Isaiah 6:8

A few minutes before noon, I got a call from the hospital next door to the church. One of our members had just entered the emergency room, and his wife was alone. "Could someone come over?" *Five pastors,* I thought, *and none in the office.* It would take a half hour for the pastor on call to make it to the ER. As I hung up, I said, "Dear God, now what?" Seconds later, I realized, *I was that someone.*

I knew Priscilla only as a member I'd see around the church. When I entered the ER waiting room, she was sitting alone with her head bowed, her fingers absently tracing the protruding veins on her other hand. "What's going on, Priscilla?" I asked as she stood for a hug. She explained that her husband had taken her for a scheduled appointment at the medical center next door and had collapsed on his way to the car. Choking back a sob, she said, "It's his heart."

We sat side-by-side silently praying. Now and then I'd touch her hand and say, "Hang in there—God's in control." After a few minutes, a doctor came and told us the damage to her husband's heart had been extensive, and then he added, "I don't think he's going to make it."

More waiting until Priscilla's family began to arrive. I slipped away and went back to my office, thanking God that he gave me the nudge it took for me to go to the hospital. The next day Priscilla and her family came to my office to make plans for her husband's funeral.

A few months after that incident, I resigned my job and moved out of town. Priscilla got my new address from the church, and at the anniversary of her husband's death wrote: *Dear Linda, You will never know how much it meant to me that you came . . . .*

Thank you, Lord, for sending me,

You Want Me To Do What?

Don't run from suffering; embrace it.
Follow me and I'll show you how. Matthew 16:25

During a staff meeting, Pastor reviewed the updated office policies. In summary, he said, "The church staff is a team, which means we help each other, and we take care of problems as they come up. If a child vomits on the floor in front of you, clean it up."

Not funny, I thought, as I remembered a little boy tossing his cookies in the waiting room of the law firm where I previously worked. Unfortunately, I was the only one available to take care of the mess.

I guessed Pastor had used the V-word scenario to point out the extremes of what any of the staff might face while working in the church. Jesus challenged his disciples to go out and care for the sick, including the lepers, and then he added, "You have been treated generously, so live generously." (Matthew 10:8)

The generous gifts I've received as a fellow worker in God's kingdom could be envied by my brothers and sisters in the secular world (maybe even my paychecks). I've been blessed to work in grace-filled churches where my perks included time off to be a room mother at my daughter's school or an extra half hour during my lunch break when an out-of-town friend came for a visit. I've had understanding and forgiving supervisors when I've overslept or had to stop at the drugstore on my way to work. Best yet, in over twenty years, I've never punched a time clock, nor have I had to clean up after a sick child!

God must smile on staffs when they function like a fine-tuned grandfather clock—its pendulum swinging with the good and not-so-good times and, at the top of each hour, playing tunes that glorify God.

Dear God, please show us how to serve you with grace,

Listen with a Cheerful Heart

A cheerful heart brings a smile to your face; a sad heart makes it hard to get through the day. Proverbs 15:13

For many years, I worked outside of my home three days a week. My neighbor, Carolyn, rarely left her home, except for when she would show up at my door for a cup of coffee on one of my days off. She'd plop down at my kitchen table and chat while our kids played in the backyard. We'd talk about our kids and things going on in the neighborhood, but after an hour my left eye would begin to twitch and frustration blushed my cheeks. I was not able to say what I was thinking: *You need to go home so I can get dinner ready for my husband and kids.*

I pondered how I could break the cycle of her stopping by, without ruining our neighborly relationship. After all, when I called Carolyn at midnight to tell her I was in labor, she was at my door in a couple of minutes to take care of my two kids.

I finally learned to take advantage of Carolyn's visit by folding clothes or ironing a few shirts. Sometimes, I stirred up a batch of brownies while we visited and served them hot out of the oven.

At work, I had a similar situation. One of my supervisors liked to sit in the chair by my desk and take a coffee break. Her visits frequently became hour-long conversations or brainstorming sessions. I'd squirm in my chair, glance at my watch, shuffle papers, and whatever I could to show I needed to get back to work. However, my supervisor didn't get the hint. One day the thought surfaced: *No chairs, no squatter!* I moved the chair into another office and no longer had to bite my tongue to keep from saying, "Don't you have work to do?"

Lord, help me be a kind listener and still get my work done,

Did you know that donuts that are made
with potato flour are called "Spudnuts"?

Florence – My Nightingale

Do you feel great? Sing. James 5:13

Florence, an elderly member of the congregation, worked in the church office every Friday morning. She'd stand near my desk to stuff bulletin material into the pre-printed covers.

I looked forward to Fridays—Florence helped keep me from falling asleep while entering 2,000 names, addresses, and baptism and confirmation dates into the new database. She'd hum or sing old favorite hymns, such as *Rock of Ages* and *What a Friend We Have in Jesus*. During holidays, she'd switch to songs of the season, *The Old Rugged Cross, Away in a Manger,* and many others. Sometimes, I'd join in and harmonize with her. I always took time to chat a bit with her, but mostly I'd listen as she told stories about her family and her faith. Florence turned Friday in to *Funday.*

One Friday, Florence didn't show up. When she didn't answer her telephone, one of the secretaries went to her home and found Florence unable to walk or talk. She had suffered a stroke. When released from the hospital, Florence moved across the state to her daughter's home and never came back to work.

I was sorry we had not been able to give Florence a farewell party. However, our chance came about two years later when Florence died, and she showed up in spirit for the memorial service. We sang her favorite songs and shared stories about the wonderful servant who'd gone home to liven up heaven with her quips, stories, and spirit-filled singing.

Years later, I find myself quoting Florence to co-workers—to lighten a stressful moment or to liven up the conversation. I wish I'd written all her little quips and stories into a journal and had them published in her memory. *First mistake I **never** made, and I'll **never** do it again,* as Florence would have said with a grin.

*Lord, thank you for being blessed by the
people we serve with in the church,*

Guide My Days

God's name is a place of protection. Proverbs 18:10

Every day is diverse and challenging when working in the church. I thought I could get a handle on my tasks when a sales representative gave me a "To Do Today" notepad. For a few days I listed projects from the most important down to the ones I hoped to look over by the end of the day. No matter how hard I tried, for every line checked off, I had as many unchecked items to move to tomorrow's list. For some projects, like organizing my pasted up hymns by the church season, tomorrow never came.

Perhaps my objectives for the day were unrealistic. By God's grace, the important stuff always got finished, even if it meant putting in some hours after the office closed.

If I had measured my success as an office administrator by the number of checkmarks on the pad by the end of each day, I'd have changed careers and become a dog walker.

Charting my workday just didn't work for me, and I have come to rely on a more user-friendly To Do Today list:

Pray for:
      1. Time
      2. Energy
      3. Resources
      4. A big dose of grace for my day

Dear God, help me to rely on your guidance
when my days seem overwhelming,

Bless My Mess

*Careful planning puts you ahead in the long run; hurry
and scurry puts you further behind.* Proverbs 21:5

I hate starting my workday with papers and pens strewn around the top of my desk. I can't think beyond the mess!

Some people can be productive under the worst of conditions. If you ask them where the month-end report is, they can slip their hands under a pile of papers and pull it out without disturbing the stack, just like a magician. If you remove something from their desk, they'll miss it immediately! I've often wondered how much time the super-sloppy staff members save by never cleaning their workspace!

I start each day with a tidy desk, but by noon half my pens and pencils have somehow jumped out of the holder and marched across the desk. File folders peek at me from open drawers, and three-ring binders stacked on the floor next to my desk resemble the Leaning Tower of Pisa.

As the worship booklets became more user friendly, I ended up with more papers and music to shuffle. It didn't take long to realize my old method of tossing everything into a folder didn't work anymore. I spent too much time searching and not enough time typing. A three-ring binder and a hole punch saved my sanity; each set of working papers for the five services had its own slot. I could flip through the pages as if I were reading a newspaper. With my new system, I was able to complete the first drafts of the bulletins more efficiently and clean up my desk before leaving for the day—to restore it to looking as if I had done nothing more than file my nails all day.

Lord of all, help me to make the best of the mess I make,

ENFJ

*It takes wisdom to build a house, and understanding to set
it on a firm foundation.* Proverbs 24:3,4

ENFJ—these letters are not a text-messaging code or an acronym
for *Exciting New Fun Job.* It's my Myers-Brigg personality test score.
According to the evaluation of the test, I am warm, empathetic,
responsive, and responsible; highly attuned to the emotional needs
and motivations of others; find potential in everyone, and want to help
others fulfill their potential. I may act as a catalyst for individual and
group growth, am loyal and responsive to praise and criticism. To top
it off, I'm sociable, facilitate others in a group, and provide inspiring
leadership. Whoa—sounds like the Myers and Brigg duo had too much
time on their hands!

I was at a dinner party recently in which this topic surfaced—I'm
an INTJ . . . . I'm an ISFJ . . . . And then someone asked, "What the
heck are you talking about?" I thought everyone knew about Myers-
Brigg and the sixteen different personality types. Some companies
rely on personality testing of some type when building a staff, because
everyone knows a company would not survive if everyone were an
ENFJ.

I need to add another characteristic to being an ENFJ—I hate
clutter. When someone tosses a stack of papers on my desk, I stop
whatever I'm doing to organize the mess (or move it out of my sight)
before I continue working. Not a big deal, but if the one doing the
tossing understood that I preferred to receive materials in batches,
neatly piled on the corner of my desk, I'd have more time to do my
work.

*Lord, thank you for creating everyone with a unique
personality to complement and enjoy each other,*

When Storms Brew

*But you—keep your eye on what you're doing; accept the
hard times along with the good.* 2 Timothy 4:5

Conflict is not new in the church. It can blow in like a *nor'easter* and suck
the joy out of an office faster than a church potluck without dessert.

In one of the churches I served, I survived a storm that gathered
strength after a well-loved pastor retired. During his long and successful
service in the church, the membership and church building had more
than doubled in size. Unfortunately, the decorations from Pastor's
farewell party had barely been taken down before a disgruntled group
of about thirty people tried to reclaim some old policies that had been
removed from their comfort zone.

For months a few members would stop by the office looking for
privileged information or wanting to vent their feelings and opinions.
I learned to listen for *sirens* to keep from being sucked into the middle
of the cyclone that would have dampened my spirit and strained my
relationship with the rest of the staff.

My line of defense to weather the storm was to adhere to the old
monkey method: *Hear no evil; speak no evil; see no evil.* I kept my ears open
for answers to prayers, my lips zipped, and my eyes on the computer
monitor, absorbed in the mission I was called to do—bulletins, office
records, finances, etc.

It took a year for *the group* to realize the congregation was planted
on solid ground and that a few thunderstorms couldn't wash away the
foundation of the church.

*Dear God, help me stay focused on my call to
support the pastors and staff in your church,*

Creative Cave

*God is bedrock under my feet, the castle in which
I live, my rescuing knight.* Psalm 17:1

The moment the Realtor showed me the den, I knew we'd found our new home. Before we sealed the deal, I put my mark on that perfect room to be my new office. It's located far away from the family room with the big-screen TV (and surround-sound speakers) and the snacks in the kitchen. I spend a lot of time in my creative cave reading and writing. I know I've hibernated too long when the big bear I live with comes in and says, "Are you going to stay in here all winter?"

On the way to my desk, I pass by a tall narrow bookcase that also serves as a meditation center. In the middle of the altar is a six-inch high wooden cross that I made as a kid in vacation church school. It's surrounded by treasures I've collected—a smooth speckled rock I picked up on the path while walking a labyrinth, a little white feather that drifted in front of me while hiking in the desert, and a *peace* candle given to me on my sixtieth birthday.

Within the reach of my long arms are all the books I use for writing and a stack of old *Writer's Digest* magazines. One wall is covered with more than a dozen framed pictures of family, friends, and vacation sites that remind me of the world outside my cave. On another wall I've hung my collection of wooden, ceramic, and metal crosses where I can see them as I work.

Over the years, I've spent about as many waking hours in an office as I have in my home. When I walk into my church office and see pictures of my family (especially the grandkids), the ceramic angel assigned to watch over my desk, and candy dish, I feel at home.

*Lord, help me make my workspace a
place to enjoy returning to each day,*

Worthless or Worthwhile?

You made all the delicate, inner parts of my body, and knit them together in my mother's womb. Psalm 139:13

I saved my vacation days for the perfect getaway—the *2000 Passion Play of our Lord* in Oberammergau, Germany. I was fortunate to be one of the two hosts on the bus filled with people from several churches, which made my trip significantly more affordable.

The two-week tour included a lot of time riding in a motor coach, which gave me the opportunity to become acquainted with the other travelers. I kept my hands busy during the miles between attractions by knitting. One day, a tourist sitting across the aisle was also knitting, and I noticed that she was watching me. Finally, she leaned over and asked, "What are you knitting?" I proudly showed her the little multicolored dishcloth under construction. She mentally turned up her nose and strongly suggested I make something worthwhile—like mittens or hats for children who have none.

For a few minutes, I wondered if I should tear apart the rag and knit a hat. I thought about all the dishrags I'd tucked into a birthday card or left at a friend's home. I decided that even though the dishrags had little value, nor would they keep little heads or pairs of hands warm, each one had been a gift from my hands, shared from my heart.

When I worked at Spirit in the Desert Retreat Center, I spent time with coordinators helping them plan their church events. I pointed out the blessings of retreating in a quiet place in the desert. As I observed groups and individuals on retreat, I sensed the Holy Spirit weaving through their lives. Without the presence of the gift of the Spirit, the retreat center would be no different than a fancy hotel—a nice place to stay, not a worthless experience, but one that falls short of the opportunity to be renewed and to grow in faith.

Gracious God, help us witness to those who feel worthless,

Why Do I Work?

*Observe people who are good at their work—skilled workers are
always in demand and admired.* Proverbs 22:29

I must admit that I am motivated to work because of the paycheck.
However, just as important as the money, I like the challenge of
learning and the way I feel when I do my job well in supporting the
rest of the staff.

I started working part-time when my kids went to school, and
over the years became a full-time workaholic. I worked mornings at
my church doing data entry and then raced across town to spend the
afternoon working in a law firm. I eventually gave up the job at church,
because the law firm *needed* me full-time, and the pay was better. Several
years later, I had serious health problems, largely due to stress on the
job. Yet, after I recuperated from surgery, I went back to the law firm
and worked even harder, trying to keep up with the never-ending
demands of the job.

One day, a former co-worker from the church where I had worked
invited me to meet her for lunch. We got about two bites into our salads
when she said, "Vuriel's retiring. I've been offered her position, and
we want you to apply for mine." She gave me the facts—I'd be making
about one-third less than my salary at the law firm, but she promised
they wouldn't make me work evenings, weekends, or take work home,
which I'd grown accustomed to.

It took a giant leap of faith to leave behind a bigger paycheck and
go back to work for the church, especially with a child in college. But
God took care of me, and my needs. Within a couple of years, I had
received a promotion, and under a revamped pay scale for support
staff, my new salary compared with what I'd been making at the law
firm.

I believe God sent Lynn to save me from self-destructing.

*Dear Lord, thank you for putting angels in my path
when I need to change directions,*

Staff Meetings

This is how everyone will recognize that you are my disciples—
when they see the love you have for each other. John 13:35

I've always had the bad habit of slipping into staff meetings just as the minute hand on the clock hit the targeted time. When I'm deep into a project, or captivated by a *creative* moment, I'm like a child watching cartoons and can't pull away to eat breakfast.

Once in the staff meeting, I'd squirm in my chair and frequently glance at my watch. The margins on the agenda become an artistic display of geometric shapes, and I mentally finish the project waiting at my desk. Before the closing prayer, I'd gather my notebook and pen and sit at the edge of my chair to make a leap out the door the moment *Amen* slipped off my lips.

When working for a large congregation, fifteen staff members gathered around the boardroom table twice a month for a meeting. I tried to get out of the meetings by whining to my supervisor. "They don't need me," I said, and she replied, "Maybe they don't need you, but you need them."

She was right. I did need the relationships I developed with my teammates in ministry. Hearing information first-hand, and being able to ask questions, saved me time and frustration. Every now and then, I'd catch a conflicting calendar item that avoided a head-on collision for the whole staff.

When I gave in to the fact that I was going to be part of the staff meetings, I actually began to enjoy the break from my desk and the extra time with the team.

Lord, I don't always have a clear picture of the whys in life.
Help me discern what's good for me,

The Lost Wallet

Rejoice with me; I have found my lost coin. Luke 15:9

I had a day off and looked forward to doing chores, running errands, and stopping by a few garage sales. First, however, I had an appointment with Lois to get my hair cut. I arrived promptly at 8:00 a.m., dropped my purse next to the chair at her station, and headed to the shampoo bay. A half hour later, I reached into my purse to pay Lois—no wallet. I dug deeper, pulled out my date book and black *Extreme Makeover* kit—no wallet! Apologetically, I looked at Lois and promised, "I'll be right back."

I raced home and searched my normal purse parking spot, but no sign of the wallet. By now, I was approaching *Panicville*. Memories surfaced from a few years earlier when my wallet had been stolen three days before Christmas from underneath my desk at church. *Could this be happening again?* I grabbed the cash in my emergency-fund envelope and counted out $18—just enough to pay for the cut, but no tip. I headed back to the beauty shop and found Lois rolling silver hair into pink plastic curlers. I slipped her the cash and babbled, "I think someone stole my wallet while we were in the back room." She kept on rolling and retorted, "Nothing's been stolen here before!"

Instead of going shopping, I went home to cancel my credit cards. As I headed for the filing cabinet, I noticed the pile of damp towels I'd dumped on the bed before dashing off to the beauty shop. Swooping them into my arms, my hand brushed across a solid mass—my wallet. I shouted "Thank you, God!" Then I thought of Lois and headed back to the beauty shop.

When Lois saw me, she put her hands on her hips and glared into my eyes. I confessed, "I found my wallet . . . will you forgive me?" She dropped her arms to her side and managed a grin. "That's what I'm supposed to do, right?"

You gave me a tip, too, God: Don't jump to conclusions,

Dwelling On Your Day

Each of you must take responsibility for doing the creative
best you can with your own life. Galatians 6:5

I don't dwell on how many times I've done the same projects week after week on the job. However, I've thought how wonderful it would be if the brain could be programmed and networked directly to the computer's processing unit to create routine documents.

Norman Vincent Peale, the author of *The Power of Positive Thinking*, suggested three ways to break out of a dull routine that may cause stress:

1. **Change your pace.** *I could try doing the bulletin backwards—start with the inserts or announcements. Maybe I should list the names of members contributing flowers for Easter and Christmas randomly instead of alphabetizing them first. Everyone would have to read through the whole list to find their names. The X, Y, Z people might like seeing their names closer to the top of the list for a change.*

2. **Seek the zest in life.** *What kind of surprises have I placed in staff mailboxes lately? A funny story? A picture of someone's new baby? Free tickets to the Cubs game? And for me, I could grab a few cut flowers from the altar bouquet left behind on Sunday and arrange them for my desk.*

3. **Forget yourself.** *How can I do that? Maybe I should put the bouquet of flowers on someone else's desk, or stop by the workroom and help the volunteers stuff a few bulletins.*

Deb, a co-worker with imagination, started the Dough-Dough Fund. When we needed to break out of our mold or to celebrate a good day, someone would grab a few dollars from the fund and go for donuts.

I'm grateful God called me to work in the church, even with the tasks I perform over and over and over.

Lord, I'm grateful for the ability to use my
skills to serve in the church office,

Advent Miracles

*God has a surprise for you: You [Mary] will become pregnant
and give birth to a son and call his name Jesus.* Luke 1:29

Advent is a short season filled with surprises and drama. The curtain
opens with two pregnant women—one "beyond her time" and the
other who had never "been with a man." The plot thickens when
Elizabeth and Zechariah name their baby John, and later when Mary
and her fiancé Joseph take off to register for the census right at the
end of her pregnancy!

The "church" sets the stage to celebrate the birth of Jesus. The
cast of characters (and some of them *are* characters) consists of normal
folks—pastors, church musicians, administrators, maintenance people,
and many volunteers. They don't have stories as amazing as Mary and
Joseph's, Elizabeth and Zechariah's, but we all have an important role
in preparing worship for Christmas.

Support staff and volunteers work hard in the office and endure
fellow workers and members who are stressed because of shopping,
making too many commitments, and not getting enough rest. One day
a crabby member complained about standing in line at the post office
for an hour. I bit my tongue and wondered, *How about me? I haven't written
a card or started my shopping. I'll be mailing packages after Christmas—again!*

The Advent scene is replayed every year in the office—the
busyness, interruptions, and surprises. Each year I rely on the magic
words, "Lord, help me!" The miracles of Christmas always happen.
By the time the last supporting cast member leaves to go home on
Christmas Eve Day, worship booklets are stacked in trays next to
boxes of little candles ready for the worshippers—and the wonder of
the *Silent Night, Holy Night* leaves me feeling blessed.

*Dear God of Advent, bless those who wait, watch,
and prepare for the celebration of the birth of Jesus,*

Out of Sight, Out of Mind

Keep a cool head. Stay alert. The devil is poised to pounce and likes nothing better than to catch you napping. 1 Peter 5:8,9

I'm fascinated with the study of the human brain—the original PC, designed by God. Every morning when the brain is *booting up,* it needs to be fed good stuff—especially protein. Drinking lattes and eating only donuts *spams* the brain and crashes the *hard drive,* and the ability to concentrate. It's quick and easy to reboot with more caffeine and the nutritionally void carbohydrates I love (anything that has *sugar* as the first ingredient on the label).

One afternoon, I nodded off at my desk and couldn't even blame the snooze on the devil. Perhaps I'd had too many evenings of basketball games and meetings, or maybe it was the tray of Christmas cookies some kind member dropped off for the staff that I couldn't pass by without sampling a few.

I have always kept a cut-glass candy dish on the corner of my desk for *guests* to enjoy. When I get busy, I tend to nibble on the candy (unless it is licorice), without giving it any thought.

A research project I read on the consumption of candy concluded that when self-diagnosed chocoholics keep an open candy dish within arm's reach, the candy is eaten in larger quantities than if the dish is covered. When the same candy is covered and placed across the room on a shelf, the consumption rate drops dramatically. Thus the case for "out of sight—out of mind."

I finally figured out that in order to get my work done efficiently, especially during the busy Advent season, I had to stay away from the cookies in the workroom and move the candy dish to the shelf across the room.

Dear Lord, help me keep my personal computer up and running, extending its life for service to you,

Christmas

*While they were there [Bethlehem], the time came for
her [Mary] to give birth.* Luke 2:6

Week after week, the church staff gives birth to projects, events, and bulletins—especially during the Christmas season. For me, each week is a 5K sprint to the finish line.

I got through the season of Christmas by *making a list, checking it twice,* and taking advantage of the willing hands of the volunteers. Ann had a way with her volunteers! They could not turn her down, knowing she would reward them with trays full of her artistically baked and decorated Christmas cookies.

No one from our staff was ever too busy to attend the annual Christmas luncheon at the pastor's home. As we arrived, we were each handed a china coffee mug filled with steaming Popcorn Tomato Soup. Then we feasted on Swedish meatballs and other traditional goodies created by the pastor's wife—her gift to the staff.

Sometimes we had an ornament exchange or drew names and shared gifts, but everyone waited for the special gift from our senior pastor. Over the years, Pastor spent time at his lake home every summer creating treasures, like a lovely wooden serving tray stenciled with angels or an old slate roof shingle decorated and personalized with everyone's last name to hang on a wall.

My all-time favorite gift received was a ten-inch wooden camel with tiny wise men pegged into three humps and a Star of the East dangling in front of the animal (to prod it along). Each of the treasures I received is the first I take out of storage after Thanksgiving and the last I put away after Epiphany—pleasant memories of working in the church office during the Christmas season.

*Dear Lord, help me to find peace during the busy holiday
season and to celebrate the birth of Christ with joy,*

SAD

*God made two big lights, the larger to take
care of the day.* Genesis 1:16

I am convinced God inspired someone to put Christmas Day on the calendar near the shortest day of the year to brighten the dark December nights. I look forward to the bright lights that adorn houses and yards during the holiday season. The color extravaganza lifts my spirits during my drive home from work. I only wish the lights could shine on until the first day of spring.

While living in the Midwest, I always dreaded the months after Christmas, especially the cloudy, cold days of January, that made the eight hours at work seem more like ten. I'd get restless, walk the hallways of the church, and end up in the copy room munching on stale Christmas cookies. By mid-afternoon, I'd have to fight the temptation to surrender to the couch in the youth room that beckoned me to lie down for a nap.

During the first winter I worked in the Valley of the Sun, I took advantage of the sixtyish-degree days and spent my lunch breaks outdoors basking in sunrays. By the end of March, I realized that I had not gone through the winter doldrums and could only conclude that while living in Illinois, I had been a victim of SAD: Seasonal Affective Disorder.

Not everyone can live in a state where the sun shines over 300 days a year! That's why brilliant engineers (perhaps from Antarctica or Norway) developed a special light-therapy lamp for people with symptoms of SAD, and why doctors sometimes have to prescribe antidepressants for those who can't shake the doldrums.

Even though the sun shines brightly in Arizona during the winter months, it is dark before I arrive home from work. I continue to wish that the holiday lights that brighten my spirits during December could shine until spring.

Dear God, shine on me during cloudy days,

Scammed in Church

No matter how cunningly he conceals his malice, eventually his evil will be exposed in public. Proverbs 26:26

A few weeks before Christmas, a woman called the office just as I was packing up to go home. She rambled on about her story: "I'm so sorry to have to ask . . . we just moved into the community and my husband needs gas to get to work . . . three little kids at home so I can't work." I was so convinced of her need that I agreed to meet her husband at a busy gas station and used my own cash to fill the tank of the minivan. He seemed shy, and could hardly look me in the eye, but thanked me several times before leaving.

About a week later, the woman came in to the office and asked if we could help to get their furniture out of storage. I told her I'd see what I could do to get the $2300. A few days later, she stopped in with the three little kids—a baby, one in pre-school, and one who just started kindergarten. They were clean and properly dressed, and their big eyes seared my heart. Once again, I was convinced of their need, made a plea on their behalf, and got a check from a special fund. When I handed her the check made out to the storage company, tears welled in her eyes as she said, "You are angels for helping my family."

It was too late to get the family on the list for the Angel Tree done by the church each year, so I told a friend about the family, and we agreed to "adopt" them. We spent one day shopping and wrapping gifts for the kids, as if they were our own grandchildren.

After Christmas, I received calls from other churches and organizations asking if we'd helped the family. They had hit up every agency, and many churches in the city, and then moved on to another community. After that incident, I decided charity should be left to the experts who don't wear their hearts on their sleeves.

Lord, help us find ways to help those with special needs,

Behind the Desk Again

*Behold, I tell you a mystery; we shall not all sleep,
but we shall all be changed!* 1 Corinthians 15:51

After being retired and roaming the USA for a year, I decided to find a part-time job. "I've done church work for over twenty years," I told my husband. "I want to do something different." I pictured myself handing out golf balls at the miniature golf course at one of our recreation centers or stocking the shelves at Kohls.

To take a break from unpacking from our trip, I picked up the free weekly newspaper and flipped through the pages, reading only the headlines. In the advertisement section, a box with bold letters caught my attention: **CHURCH SECRETARY WANTED.** I read it with the same normal curiosity I'd always had about what kinds of jobs were available in the market. *That will make a nice job for someone,* I thought and tossed the newspaper into the recycling pile.

Another day, and in another local newspaper, I saw the same box. This time I read the ad more intentionally. The deadline to apply was April 10. I looked at the calendar—tomorrow. *But what do I care?* I thought. *I'm not going to work in the church again.*

The next morning I awoke thinking about that job. However, we had gotten rid of our second car, and if I went back to work, there would be days I'd have to get there on foot or drive the golf cart (allowed on Sun City streets). I pulled up the name of the church on the website and found it: 103rd and Boswell, Sun City—less than two miles from my house.

I polished up an old resume and attached it to an e-mail file with a little note: "This ad just kept surfacing. I see it as a sign that God wants me to apply." A week later I began the perfect post-retirement job, working four mornings a week!

*Lord, thank you for boldly nudging me to do what I love,
serving in the church as part of the support staff,*

A Day in the Church Office

On a good day, enjoy yourself; on a bad day, examine your conscience. Ecclesiastes 7:14

Today's Schedule:

8:00	Devotions with support staff
8:15	Check e-mail
8:30	Sort projects from old to new
10:00	Coffee break
10:15	Start projects left over from last week
12:00	Lunch
1:00	Begin new projects for week
3:00	Coffee break
3:15	Wrap up projects
4:45	Tidy up desk before going home

Today went perfectly! No interruptions by deliverymen or stragglers from Women's Bible Study "to see how I'm doing." The copy machine behaved itself and a fresh pot of coffee and a chocolate donut awaited me for my morning coffee break!

By noon I'd delivered to the accountant the report that had been due Friday. I met a friend for lunch and arrived early! The afternoon slipped by as if I was at a chic flick. I had a little strut to my step as I placed the first draft of the bulletin into Pastor's box for proofing. (Reminder: Send a thank you memo to everyone for getting their information in on time!) I ran into Pastor during my afternoon break, and he bragged about how nice last Sunday's bulletin looked. Before going home, I tidied up my desk and polished it for the first time in years! And the best part—I left the office at exactly 5:00!

Dear Lord, forgive me for dreaming. Help me remember how boring perfect days in the office would be,

The "Mis-Gift"

[God's wisdom is] . . . what God determined as the way to bring out his best in us, long before we ever arrived on the scene. 1 Corinthians 2:10

As a gift for my first anniversary working for the church, I received a plant for my office. Brilliant yellow blooms on tall stems peeked through rich green, almost heart-shaped, leaves. I read the tag—*Calla lily; plant in sunny location. Preferred temperature 50-70 degrees. Keep soil moist.*

I left my plant at work, where I spend more concentrated time than any other place during the week, and each morning upon my arriving, it greeted me like a ray of sun. But within a few days the leaves started to turn brown and the blossoms began to fade. I began cutting off the decaying parts at the base of the plant until it looked like a hungry deer or rabbit had invaded my office.

The plant no longer gave me pleasure. *Dear God,* I prayed, *what am I doing to kill this beautiful creation?* I removed the instruction tag and read it again. *50-70 degrees; moist soil.* I live in the desert. The humidity in and outdoors ranges from seven to ten percent most of the year. The air conditioner system is timed to run only when the office is occupied. The rest of the time, the office is a stifling eighty-plus degrees. *Poor little plant,* I thought, *you don't belong in Arizona! Especially in my hands that have no green thumbs.* I took the plant to my house—a much better fit.

The "mis-gifted" plant is similar to staff members I've worked with, such as a receptionist with anger issues, a fast keyboarder who suffers mental anguish each month while producing the newsletter, and a shopaholic, whose favorite store is OfficeMax.

Lord, create in us a spirit of understanding, flexibility,
and acceptance of the gift needed to serve you,

Amazing Grace

And the grace of God was on him. Luke 2:40

Every day I learn something new while working in the church office, which proves you *can* teach an old dog new tricks! Last week I learned you cannot take information received on its face value. I e-mailed a worship booklet to a guest minister so she could provide me with the responsive prayer, Scripture lessons, sermon title, and hymns. She added the information directly into the Word document and returned it to me.

I eyeballed the bulletin for errors. *Looks good,* I thought, and printed it for Bob, my 91-year-old copy guy, to produce. He finished copying the regular bulletins and made twenty-five large-print copies. When he dug into the three-ring binder of hymns already enlarged, he said, "None of the hymns listed in the bulletin are in this book. Please type them for me." I scratched my head and wondered why the verses to "What a Friend We Have in Jesus" and "Amazing Grace" had never been typed before. I checked the file: Page 507—not "What a Friend." Page 507—not "Amazing Grace." Then bells went off in my head. The pastor had used a different hymnal when selecting the hymns! The churches I had worked for before had all used the same hymnal, and it didn't occur to me to cross-reference the songs with the hymnal stored above my desk.

There weren't enough preprinted covers to reprint the booklet, so I notified the worship leader she'd have to *right* the wrong page numbers by making an announcement before each hymn. "No problem," she said. Another day of amazing grace in the church office.

*Dear Lord, thank you for the daily dose of grace that
we receive in our waking breath,*

Baby in Wedding?

Make the most of every opportunity. Be gracious in your speech.
Colossians 4:6

I enjoyed being the wedding coordinator for our large congregation. We'd have about thirty weddings a year, and I had the privilege of working with a lot of wonderful couples as they began their life together. Most of the couples were members of the congregation, but occasionally I'd get a phone call, "Do you perform marriage services for nonmembers?" I figured that by the time they had reached the letter "O" under *Churches* in the yellow pages, they had received a lot of rejections, so I listened to their story, and then I'd tell them our policy.

"Our church is a family," I'd say, "and because you would not want to barge in on a family event without an invitation, you will need to come to church at least one time. After church introduce yourself to the pastor and tell him that you'd like to be married in this church."

At the initial meeting with a nonmember couple, the nineteen-year-old bride said, "We'd like to have our ten-month-old little boy serve as the ring bearer and come down the aisle in a baby walker."

I visualized a baby stuffed into a tuxedo, playing bumper cars with the pews as he processed down the aisle, flinging the ring pillow aside, and a frustrated grandpa coercing him to the altar while dragging a frantic bride behind him. Thankfully, God took control of my tongue. I choked back a chuckle and replied, "That's a pretty clever idea, but weddings can be very stressful."

Fortunately, one of the grandmothers held the little "ring bearer" in her lap, and the bride's father escorted his daughter down the aisle without incident.

Lord, help us to act graciously as we work with your children,

Blessings

Blessed the man, blessed the woman, who listens to me, awake and ready for me each morning, alert and responsive as I start my day's work. Proverbs 8:34

Last winter the son of one of my classmates died after a long confinement following an accident. His mother, Kay, went through months of gray days, lacking joy in her life. One morning Kay pledged to herself that she would share three blessings every day on her Facebook page. They started out pretty basic, but over the weeks I could see that her blessings included many things she had enjoyed before her son died. As a result of her sharing, many of her Facebook friends were inspired and began to recite their own blessings.

There are days my three blessings might read like this: (1) I made it to work on time, (2) I remembered to bring my lunch, and (3) I got through the day without a headache.

It's difficult to feel blessed every day, especially when people in our family, neighborhood, or even in the church, freely unload their negative opinions, fears, and angst on us. And if on the way to work you tune the radio to a news station, a cloud may follow you to work and hang over your desk. That's when we need to look for blessings to help the sun shine through the clouds.

God doesn't say blessings have to be a big deal, but he does say that we should give thanks for all things. Thank you, Kay, for reminding us that by naming a blessing—two or three—it becomes a good way to start or end each day.

Lord, may we turn to you when we need help feeling blessed,

On one of his expeditionary missions, noted donut lover
Admiral Richard Byrd took along 100 barrels of flour
which was enough to make donuts for two years.

Crazymakers

Is it any wonder that people go crazy right and left?
Ecclesiastes 9:3

Do you get worn out or drained by co-workers or friends who are reeling out of control most of the time? A few years ago I took a class based on Julia Cameron's book *An Artist's Way . . . a Spiritual Path to Higher Creativity*. Cameron referred to people in our lives who create excess stress as "crazymakers."

The interesting thing is that a crazymaker is out of control in her or his life and is bent on trying to make you crazy, too. They'll hog your time, put you in the middle of a conflict, and never take responsibility for their own actions. Crazymakers could win an Academy Award for best actor and nominate you for best supporting actor. Your time will be wasted because they have no schedule, nor do they have any sense of organization. Don't get me wrong—crazymakers can be a lot of fun for a while, but need to be caged and let out only to do their job!

My crazymaker was my co-worker at a retreat center. Carrie often came to work already frustrated from the commute or from her boyfriend who was a co-crazymaker. One day I asked Carrie about the progress she was making on getting a group registered for an event. I must have hit her last nerve. She flew out from behind the receptionist desk, swung her arms over her head, and shook her head until I thought her long brown hair would braid itself. After the tantrum, she went back to work as if nothing had happened. From that day on I watched for signs—jaws locked, eyes squinting, chest heaving—before I approached her with a hot topic.

Dear God, fortify me with the wisdom and the patience I need to work with crazymakers. By your grace, may I never become one,

Doodling

Let's leave the preschool finger-painting exercises on Christ and get on with the grand work of art. Grow up in Christ. Hebrews 6:1

Art therapy is one of the recommended ways to de-stress. A long telephone conversation brings out my creative doodling. The masterpiece starts in the middle of the page, and by drawing basic shapes of squares, diamonds, circles, and then adding leaves and some spears of grass at the base, I come up with a unique flower in a garden. If I were to get my highlighter out and color it, I might even consider framing it for a wall in the nursery.

Art therapy is used to encourage patients to express themselves when something is too painful to talk or write about. Therapists use drawings, paintings, or other art media to find out what's going on with their patients and then to treat them.

I've come up with some do-it-yourself art projects to help release stress on the job:

- Use your pencil and trace objects from your desk to decorate your desk calendar.
- Use colorful construction paper to cut out random shapes to use as notepaper.
- Schedule a finger-painting session during lunch breaks on casual-dress Fridays.
- Make a collage of notes from people who drive you crazy and then shred it!

What artistic ways have you created to lay out the newsletter to make it more interesting to read, or to stack reams of copy paper in rows on a shelf so that a finger can reach in between each stack for easy removal, or to make Christmas cookies that actually resemble a wise man bearing gifts?

Lord, help us use the gifts we've been given, before the glittering wrapping paper begins to fade,

A-Camping We Will Go

*Even when the way goes through Death Valley, I'm not
afraid when you walk at my side.* Psalm 23:4

I flipped through the registration forms submitted for summer Bible camp and let the memories of my only camping experience roll through my mind. I had been twelve years old and ten miles from home. For an instant, I could smell the stinky athletic shorts, tee shirts, and muddy tennis shoes that I dragged home in my little cardboard suitcase. Fifty years later a pang of homesickness hit my stomach as if I'd just watched my parents drive away from the camp. I could almost taste the tears that had silently dripped on my pillow—my only comfort from home.

My childhood church made sure every child could go to camp, like other churches where I have worked. My parents gladly accepted the scholarship that made it possible for me to go to Riverside Bible Camp—a place carved out of a few acres of precious Iowa farm and woodland.

The loneliness lasted a couple of days until my heavenly Father came to visit me as I wandered through the woods, sang and prayed in the chapel, splashed in the pool, sat around the dinner table giggling with new friends, looked into the eyes of the counselors, and learned more about Jesus. I can't say that the week was a spiritual high or that I had an awakening or out-of-body experience, but it gave me a foundation to carry me throughout my faith journey.

I'm grateful that churches continue to value camping for kids (and adults). I think I'll check the registration for next year. Maybe they would take a sixty-five-year old kid!

*Dear Father, I remember when you came to me at camp.
Thank you for following me in my faith journey,*

The Gift of Energy

That's why I'm [Paul] working so hard at day after day, year after year,
doing my best with the energy God so graciously gives me. Colossians 1:29

God graciously gave us the gift of spiritual and physical energy the moment we inhaled our first breath of air. Unlike the Energizer® bunny that just keeps on going, our energy needs to be renewed on a regular basis.

I used to go to work on Monday mornings exhausted, until I realized that my three children (and husband) didn't care if their shirts were pressed, if the cookies in their lunch box were freshly out of the oven, and that no matter how many hours I spent cleaning and fussing in the kitchen over the weekend, I'd never win a Good Housekeeping award.

Look around your office. Do you see co-workers yawning, sighing, or propping their heads up while they work? Do their eyes lack luster? Do they appear to be working like robots, lacking joy in their ministry? Maybe it's time to open the full-service body and mind station and offer overhauls. Some common energy-depleting activities to try to avoid:

- Sleep deprivation: Adults need seven or eight hours of sleep every night.
- Poor eating habits: The body needs fruit, vegetables, lean meat, and whole grains to function.
- Working without a break: A short break gives the body and mind a boost for the rest of the day.
- Lacking priorities for the day: Put "nurturing body, mind, and soul" on your agenda each morning.
- Harboring anger or frustration: Pray for wisdom and direction to resolve personal matters.

Dear God, remind me that prayer helps to renew energy,

God Opens and Closes Doors

Open any door and keep it open, lock any door
and keep it locked. Isaiah 22:23

I believe God calls us to work in the church office just like ordained ministers and program staff. I also believe that God closes doors on bad jobs and opens a door for one that is better suited for our skill level, temperament, and health.

For many years, I served as the office manager for a fast-paced small law firm. One day while talking to one of my bosses, I felt something in my abdomen pop. Instantly a pain sliced through my body, paralyzing me from my waist to my left shoulder. After a trip to the ER, it took weeks of testing and no results until another "pop" and a diagnosis that ulcers had formed in my stomach and perforated through the lining. The surgeon removed two-thirds of my stomach.

After recovering from surgery, I returned to my desk and got right back into the same stressful work. After a few months, I knew I didn't want to give the firm the rest of my stomach and went back to work for the church where I'd served earlier. As with any new position, I had many overwhelming days, I worked unsolicited overtime hours, telling myself, "It's okay, because it's my church—sort of like volunteering." I fell into the bad habit of eating lunch at my desk, skipping breaks, and taking work home.

I had back-pedaled on the pledge I had made to God that I would never worship my work again. I took time to get organized in my office and to become better acquainted with the great staff members. We became a team and helped each other. My workload became manageable, and I became better at closing the door on my day and going home at 5:00 p.m.

"God closes doors no man can open and
God opens doors no man can close." (Unknown)
Thank you, God, for opening a double-wide door for me,

God's Hand

*Never walk away from someone who deserves help; your
hand is God's hand for that person.* Proverbs 3:27

On my first secretarial job, I worked at a county welfare office as a
clerk typist. I assisted three caseworkers by transcribing case histories
and filling out forms. One afternoon, my husband, Glen, came into
the office with a long face and told me I needed to leave with him. I
grabbed my purse and signed out for the day.

As soon as we got outside, he said, "There's been an accident.
We need to get to Mom's house." Later we learned that his father and
younger brother had been killed—heroes for trying to save another
guy during a dirt cave-in on a sewer-construction project.

I received sympathy cards from co-workers. The office sent a
bouquet of flowers to the funeral home. A week later, I returned
to work tired and tender. After co-workers uttered sympathies like
the ones I'd grown numb from hearing all week, I went to the work
cupboard. There I found a new stack of files and dictated tapes shoring
up the files I'd left behind. I grabbed a stack of work and headed to my
desk. For the rest of the day, I fought tears to keep them from spoiling
my original documents and the four carbon copies I'd transcribed with
my heavy hands and heart. My boss and co-workers just didn't get it. I
needed someone to show they cared by lightening my workload.

Years later, my elderly mother-in-law passed away after a lengthy
illness. I took a week off to go to the memorial service and help close
out her home. When I returned to the church office, I expected to put
in extra time to get the newsletter out on time. But when I pulled up
the file on the computer, the newsletter was done—a gift from my
boss.

*Dear God, thank you for co-workers who
graciously give of their time when needed,*

Hang in There

*They hang their life from one thin thread, they hitch
their fate to a spider web.* Job 8:14

"We must, indeed, all hang together, or most assuredly we shall
all hang separately."—Benjamin Franklin (just before
signing the Declaration of Independence, 1776)

I saw a picture of a kitten clutching a frail twig on a branch. That's
how my new assistant, Sherry, must have felt when she started her job.
She'd never worked in a church office and, with her eyes sparkling, she
said, "It will be fun working in a church!"

I'd polished her desk, refreshed the supply of paper clips, pens,
pencils, and checked the stapler to make sure it worked without
jamming. I gifted her with a new two-tiered in-and-out box where she
could reach it without getting off her chair. She sat down and adjusted
her chair, and then I gave her a quick tour of the building. I showed
her where supplies were stored, pointed out the light switches for the
entrances and rooms, and told her where we gathered for breaks and
lunch.

I staged a phone call to show her our cheerful answering practice:
"Good morning, Our Saviour's. My name is Linda. How may I help
you?" and then how to put a call on hold or forward it on. She had
the "I'm ready to tackle this job" look on her face, so I left her alone
for a few minutes to get a feel for the office and to peruse the files in
her desk.

A few minutes later, I returned with a stack of reality—last
Sunday's attendance sheets and fourteen new-member intake forms
to be entered into the database. Within a flash, the confident smile
turned to panic, "Enough for now!"

*Dear God, thank you for helping us survive our first days,
weeks, and months in the church office,*

Crucified

Have some of you noticed that we are not yet perfect?
(No great surprise, right?) Galatians 2:17

I sat through a staff meeting and contributed only when asked about a calendar event. Afterward my co-worker, Carole, asked, "Okay, what's wrong? You were way too quiet in the meeting, and I want to know what's going on." I choked back a sob trying to surface and told her my story.

"I missed putting June's article about the new circle being formed in the newsletter," I said, and then I watched for her response.

"Not June's!" she said, and put her hands together as if to offer a silent prayer. June had a reputation for being on top of everything and always got her articles in on time.

"Get over it, Linda," she said. "It's not a big deal. She'll forgive, and forget. Remember, no one's perfect!"

It wasn't a big deal for us, but it was a BIG deal to June. Besides, I liked June and hated the fact that I had let her down.

I'd awakened on Sunday morning with a premonition that the monthly newsletter went out without June's article. When I checked the newsletter, I went from anxious to panic in less than a second. I e-mailed June to ease her into the disappointment and to offer any help to advertise her event. *Surely, she'd understand the omission and forgive me,* I thought. *After all, this is the church.*

There was no forgiveness in her reply. She said, "You need to get organized . . . a notebook to put drafts into." But it was the last sentence that broke my spirit: "You are a paid employee—we expect more of you!"

I thumbed through the three-ring binder, labeled NEWSLETTER, and said, "I guess I need to do even more . . . perhaps a monthly index sheet to record articles I receive" . . . . And, then I gave *it* to God to resolve.

Dear God, you know we're not perfect in the church office,

Is It I, Lord?

"I'll go. Send me!" Isaiah 6:8

A member of the congregation called to tell me that for the past two weeks the lyrics in the closing hymn in the bulletin were incorrect. "The song goes, *Here I am, Lord, it is I, Lord,* not *is it I, Lord?*"

Before he called the office, he said he had referred to the hymnal from his previous church and in that book the words read, "It is I, Lord." It had been one of his favorite songs and he had memorized it that way. Then he said, "I wonder why there is a question mark at the end of the sentence?"

I put on my detective hat and pulled out the hymnal used for worship services and verified that I had typed it as printed in that book. When I called the member back, and told him the good news, he replied, "Well, your hymnal must be wrong."

Often there is more than one way to say something. Look at the four Gospels. The same incident frequently was reported by more than one writer—all with a different slant. None of the four Gospels were certified as the "true" one. It's the message that is important to the reader.

All day long the words and tune to the wonderful hymn rolled through my head. Every time I got to the phrase "Is it I, Lord?" I gladly said, "Yes!"

Later I searched the web to check the hymn from a trusted source, but couldn't get the words without paying a fee. That afternoon at home I couldn't resist checking the church hymnal from another church and found the word *is* instead of *it*. I decided *is* stays in the bulletin, and even if *is* is wrong, it is right.

Dear Lord, here I am—ready to serve you in every opportunity that arises during the day,

Happy and Content, Most of the Time

Help others with encouraging words; don't drag them down by finding fault. Romans 14:19

"I am happy and content because I think I am."
—Alain-Rene Lesage

It has been five years since my husband, Glen, and I went through a year of marriage adjustment. Our therapist sent us home with a book: *Getting the Love You Want*, written by Harville Hendrix, Ph.D. The author challenged us to go back through our marriage to get to know each other all over again—a big challenge after thirty-nine years. I'd spent a good deal of those years smiling on the outside and seething on the inside, stacking resentment in my mind like a mile-high sub sandwich. Fortunately, my husband and I were able to work through the gripes, grievances, and discovered values and joys we had shared—plus a whole lot of love.

As full-time employees, we spend almost as many hours each day in our offices as we do at home. It's easy for co-workers to experience misunderstandings, especially during the busy seasons of the church year. Issues left to fester can affect the "marriage" of the entire staff. The Bible tells us to go directly to the person with whom we have a gripe, and if that doesn't work, to take it to a mediator—a pastor or church administrator—to resolve the issue.

During marriage therapy, I learned that instead of building a case in my mind against my husband, I needed to step back and examine if my expectations for our relationship were reasonable and something we could both agree to. After getting my personal life in order, everything at work went better, too, and I *am* happy and content.

Dear Father, help us to find a happy and contented place at home and in the office,

Healthy Choices

If you grow a healthy tree, you'll pick healthy fruit. Matthew 12:33

We get a day off for Presidents' Day, Independence Day, Veterans Day, and many other traditional holidays. I'm advocating a *Mental Health Day* and an *Attitude Adjustment Day*. There are no holidays in June or August, so let's petition to get two more days off during the summer!

I worked in a law office in which the staff helped write the office policy manual. We removed the sick-day provision and gave ourselves twelve *Healthy Choice Days* (not to be confused with vacation days), which could not be accumulated to use for a long weekend away from the office. When a Healthy Choice Day was requested, or if someone called in at 8:05 a.m. and requested a day off under the HCD policy, no questions were asked. When an employee reached the twelve-day limit, additional days off were taken as unpaid leave.

This policy worked in the office because everyone valued his or her job and the relationship they had with each other. Staff members used their HCD days to take care of themselves physically, mentally, and emotionally. The office thrived, too, with more productive, dependable, healthier, and happier employees.

In the church office, it's common for one staff member to assist several pastors or program staff members. If you're overwhelmed by 8:05 a.m., perhaps you qualify for a Healthy Choice Day off.

Dear Lord, help us take care of our bodies, minds, and souls,

"Between the optimist and the pessimist, the difference is droll.
The optimist sees the doughnut; the pessimist the hole!"
—Oscar Wilde

Herding Cats

These are the numbers of those registered by Moses and Aaron,
registered with the help of the leaders of Israel, twelve men,
each representing his ancestral family. Numbers 1:44

Making a list, checking it twice . . . . No, it's not Christmas. It's Parochial Report time!

The responsibility for getting the annual parochial report completed and sent to the national church office came with my job description. Every year I tried to give the task away, but no one volunteered to tackle the multi-paged form that needed several people to submit data to be consolidated into one legible report.

The first year I had to hunt down reports from all the staff members already buried to their knees in their ministry programs. I missed the April 1 deadline, which didn't sit well with me because I've always taken pride in being responsible, organized, and efficient (the work ethic of trying to please everyone all the time).

When I received the report the following year, I made copies for each department and attached a note: "Please mark your calendar. This report is due by April 1. I need your piece of the puzzle completed and in my box by March 15, or I will camp at your door until I receive it."

As the reports dribbled in, I processed them in between my routine projects and never felt overwhelmed. Even with the threat of camping at office doors, the report was mailed to the national office a few days late. I decided that herding cats might be easier than gathering reports from busy people.

We know that no church office is *purr-fect* and that only God can herd cats.

Lord, help me remember that I am not in control of everything,

The Revolving Door

He doesn't play hide-and-seek with us. He's not remote; he's "near."
Acts 17:28

From this scripture, you might think that Paul was writing about a church administrator, or pastor, instead of God.

For years, I worked with Sally, who served as the church administrator. Sally had an open-door policy—some days more like a revolving-door opportunity for the staff to unload frustration or to upload information that she kept in a mental filing cabinet.

One late October evening, my daughter Susan, who was a junior in high school, came home all excited. "Mom, Dad, there's a foreign-exchange student in my school who needs a new host family. Please, can Berkin come to live with us?"

Our household had shrunken down to one child. I wasn't sure if I had enough energy for another teenager to live with us until the end of the school year. However, after meeting the lovable Turkish young man, we invited him to move into the guest bedroom.

It didn't take long to realize that my home had many revolving doors. I'd become like Sally. Berkin had questions—all of which had an urgent tone. He needed help planning outings to indoctrinate him into American culture. He couldn't drive, so I took my fair share of turns driving him to the train station, mall, to a friend's house, or to activities at school. Loneliness, fear, or frustration surfaced and turned into late-night mom-and-son conversations.

When Berkin went back to Istanbul, he left a hole in my heart. Soon everything I'd put on the back burner for eight months filled the hole. Two years later, we took another exchange student—Andrea from Switzerland—and the doors revolved again for another year.

Dear God, may we always keep the door open to ministry
inside and outside of the church office,

Holding My Tongue

*Some were yelling one thing, some another. Most of them had no
idea what was going on or why they were there.* Acts 19:32

My favorite way to start the day is on my patio with a cup of tea, a
bowl of oatmeal, and my basket of goodies—a copy of *The Message*
Bible, a daily devotional booklet from my church, a journal, and an
inspirational book, such as *Simple Abundance: A Daybook of Comfort and
Joy* written by Sarah ban Breathnach. This quiet time strengthens my
spirit for the rest of the day.

Before I eat, I toss a couple of handfuls of birdseed on the rocky
landscaping and watch the doves, quails, and sparrows scratch and
scrap for their share of food. Lately they've been fighting with each
other for their shares of seed. If you read newspaper editorials or watch
TV news, you'll notice that human beings can't get along much better
than my fine-feathered friends can.

One day I accompanied a fire inspector around the office for his
semi-annual inspection of the batteries for the emergency exit lights
and other fire hazards. After covering the whole building, he followed
me back to the office to complete his report.

Before leaving, this friendly inspector started a new conversation
that went from "It's sure hot for March" to bashing a prominent
government official. When he repeated a rumor that had circulated
freely over the Internet, I had all I could do to keep from screaming,
"Stop! You don't know what you're talking about!" But the Speaker of
the [church] House intervened and guided my tongue. "I'll pretend like
I didn't hear you say that," I said, and the conversation ended.

*Dear Lord, help us learn how to deal with
opposition and difficult people,*

It's Not My Job

Their job is to carry The Dwelling and all its furnishings,
maintain it, and camp around it. Numbers 1:50

The pastor leaves for a month's vacation and inevitably, something (or someone) needs special attention within the first forty-eight hours. Most recently, the chiller in our air-conditioning system (challenged to regulate the temperature in the building to a cool 75 degrees when the outside temperature is over 105) also went on vacation. During the Sunday worship service, the bulletin served a dual purpose as a handheld fan.

On Monday morning, Staffer A e-mailed Staffer B and asked B to order service for the air conditioning. Staffer A copied Staffer C (me) that the process was underway to get the chiller fixed. By Wednesday there had been no signs of anyone with a tool bag and testing equipment, and I began to picture the church service the following weekend being moved to the fellowship hall and how this would affect many of the seniors who don't like to worship from anywhere but their regular pew. Some would prefer to sweat it out!

I called the service company to find out when we might be seeing a tech and was told, "Sorry, we haven't received an order." I begged her to send someone out as soon as possible. I followed up the call with a note to Staffer B and told him that I'd taken care of the service order and copied Staffer A.

I wondered, *If it wasn't A's job, or B's job, then whose job is it?* In the end, it doesn't matter who makes the call. It's everyone's job to make sure the conditions are right to worship God.

Dear Father, I'm willing to do whatever it takes to make the
church run more smoothly, but I need to know who's in charge,

Junk Pens

God is sheer mercy and grace; not easily angered, he's rich in love.
Psalm 103:8

I'm snobbish about ink pens. I buy my favorite stick pen, which costs more than a dime, by the dozens. It fits perfectly in my hand, glides over paper like an ice skater, and brings smudge-free words to life.

One day while I stood by the mailboxes in our office, I grabbed a pen from the coffee cup that held about a dozen odd pens and pencils and began to write a message to the maintenance man. The pen either had dried up or had gone on strike. I went on a warpath to find a pen that would write. If it didn't write within the first three letters, I tossed it into the garbage. Five pens later, I found one that wrote on the second letter.

Later that night, I sat at my husband's computer desk and picked up a pen to sign a check, clicked it, and then glided the tip of the pen across the paper. No ink. As I aimed the pen at the garbage can, Glen said, "Hey, that's my favorite pen. You can't throw it away!"

"How can you put up with a pen that won't write on command?" I asked, and handed it over to him. He grabbed the defenseless pen and forced the tip on to a piece of scrap paper. "You go like this," he said, and scribbled a few phantom lines, shook the pen a few times, and on the third scribble actually produced a legible signature. "Good as new," he smiled.

I shook my head and said, "I guess you are more patient with weak and afflicted pens than I am." That should not have surprised me—he's put up with all my imperfections for over forty-five years.

Dear Lord, thank you for being a patient God and for giving me more than one chance to get things right,

It's the Pits

They trip on ropes they've hidden, and fall into pits they've dug themselves.
Job 18:10

On busy workdays, I often leave my office only when nature calls, and then I wonder why I'm exhausted at the end of the day. When a project is going smoothly, and *it will only take a few minutes to complete*, it's easy to get into pitfalls. A few I've perfected during my career:

- Ignoring breaks. Breaks refresh the mind and the body. Many states in the U.S. have included paid breaks in their labor-law policies; most employers recommend this practice.
- Eating lunch at your desk. Working through lunch not only keeps you from socializing with co-workers in the lunchroom, it also lessens your enjoyment of the food you are eating and can cause overeating.
- Snacking on sugary treats while working. Do you ever wonder who ate all the M&Ms in the candy dish on your desk? Try adding a mixture of healthy nuts—almonds, cashews, walnuts—to sweet treats, and limit this snack to one handful a day.
- Working overtime—unauthorized and unpaid. Telling yourself "I work for my church, and it's part of my ministry." Working overtime without documenting the hours can lead to a continually overworked employee.

One evening I drove home from a long day of work and couldn't remember which route I'd driven. But I had finished the report my boss had asked for, and I knew he'd be happy to see it on his desk when he arrived the next morning. He might not have been happy with me if he'd seen me driving home under the influence of no breaks during the day.

Lord, remind me how Jesus pulled away from his ministry to be refreshed,

Life of Riley

*God spoke: "Swarm, Ocean, with fish and all sea life! Birds,
fly through the sky over Earth!"* Genesis 1:20

"This is the life of Riley," I said, while I stretched out in a lounge chair
on my daughter's spacious porch. I looked at the mountain in the west
and listened to birds singing and crickets calling out from all angles
of the yard.

"Just who is Riley?" Karen asked.

"I don't know," I admitted.

It's a phrase I borrowed from my mother. After lunch, whenever
the Iowa summer weather permitted, she'd stretch out on a lounge
chair on the porch and say, "This is the life of Riley." She'd stare at the
clear sky, breathing in the fresh air, and succumb to a catnap before
going back to her chores.

Whoever Riley is, he must know how to relax and enjoy the sweet
things in life.

After my daughter had her last baby, I took time away from my job
to give her a hand with household chores and her Nate—not yet two
years old. After lunch, when Karen, Baby Mason, and Nate took a nap,
I'd ditch the cleaning and laundry and head for the porch for *Riley* time
to meditate and write in my journal. Like my mother, I'd doze off for
a while and awaken ready to tackle another load of laundry and push
Nate around the porch on his "motorcycle."

Don't wait until you're a grandparent, or almost retired, to
experience the *life of Riley*. When the weather permits, break loose from
your office. Go outside. Breathe in the freshness of the day, or listen
to children playing, and dogs barking. Watch a squirrel flash its tail to
the sun or a stream of jet vapor disintegrate across the sky.

Thank you, God, for giving us opportunities to be refreshed,

Locking Up

Jesus came through the locked doors, stood among them,
and said, "Peace to you." John 20:26

When was the last time you locked your office door on a Friday afternoon and whispered a prayer, "I've done all I could this week, Lord. See you Monday!"

Friday is a good day to do a personal performance review for the week you've just gone through.

1. Did I interact with co-workers, with walk-in visitors? Were my words gentle or sarcastic?
2. Is there a better way to deal with the vendor who messed up my order?
3. Did I spend enough time, or too much time, in conversation with the member whose husband had a stroke and can no longer converse with her?
4. Did I hold my tongue when I overheard someone gossiping or being rude?
5. When I bypassed training on a new program, and struggled through it without making progress, did I admit that maybe I need to ask for help?
6. Were my expectations for the week realistic?
7. Did I remember to back up the computer system?
8. Did I help someone meet his or her personal goal?
9. Did I color outside the lines or dangle my feet and arms outside the box to try something new?
10. Did I seek help or advice from my supervisor, co-workers, or from the Master Key Holder?

Dear God, by your grace, we get to start over every day,

"Loose Lips Sink Ships"

Post a guard at my mouth, God, set a watch at the door of my lips.
Psalm 141:3

"Loose lips sink ships" is my brother Gary's favorite saying when he hears someone gossiping or repeating sensitive information. It is easy to get caught up in conversations that lead toward the direction of becoming gossip, or are in the category of "What happens in Vegas stays in Vegas."

When the only thing two people have in common is that they work together in an office, it's easy to get caught up in conversation about people and events of the church.

Recently I had lunch with a co-worker. After returning to my desk, I thought about the conversation we'd had about a member of the church and began to feel as if I had betrayed my lips. We didn't talk about anything that wasn't common knowledge, but it just didn't feel right with my soul.

To keep from having another episode of loose-lip syndrome during lunch with a co-worker, I developed a menu of appropriate behavior:

1. *Appetizer*: Light conversation about the weather, the atmosphere of the restaurant, the prompt service;
2. *Entrée*: Topics that could be published on the front page of the church newsletter;
3. *Dessert*: Sweet stories of blessings in our lives;
4. *Bill*: Pay it forward—What I've learned that can make a difference in my own life that I can share with others; and
5. *Tip*: A quote from my mother: Mind my Ps and Qs, which I've interpreted as: practice prudence, positivity, playfulness, peaceful sharing, and quit talking so much and listen more.

Lord, when I'm vulnerable, post a guard on my lips,

Disney World

I'm caught in a maze and can't find my way out, blinded by tears of pain and frustration. Psalm 88:9

Our jobs keep us away from our "other life" about eight hours a day or less, if blessed to work part-time. That means we have approximately sixteen hours a day to be influenced by family, friends, inconsiderate people, such as the piggyback driver who rides your bumper on the way to work.

Have you ever felt like climbing back under the covers of your unmade bed by the time the kids are dressed, everyone's been "kissed-off" to school or work, and you've found the earrings that match your outfit? If so, you've already been on a roller-coaster ride before your workday started.

I am usually prepared for whatever hits my desk during the day, except for when the telephone rings at 9:00 a.m. and I hear, "Linda, this is Bill. I'm running a fever and won't be able to run the newsletter today." That's when I go on another roller-coaster ride while trying to answer phones, sign for deliveries, and armwrestle the duplicating machine. When I start searching the office for something chocolate to eat, I know I'm like a car with no brakes and I'm sure to crash.

We are called to serve in the church office, not in Disney World, where all rides are fun. When a morning starts in a stressful manner, perhaps we need to start the day over. Imagine putting on your coat, grabbing your workbag (which you just filled with frustration), and going home. Then before driving back to work picture stopping at Starbuck's and enjoying a cup of coffee or tea. Upon entering your office, you pause and ask God to take away any stress that you put upon yourself. Then dump the contents of your workbag at the feet of Jesus and say "Amen."

Lord, help me enter my office each day with an empty workbag and a willing heart,

More Stress

Take this cup away from me. Mark 14:36

Not another story about stress, you might be thinking. Because stress on the job is one of the biggest complaints I hear when talking with other church employees (or from those who work in secular offices), please bear with me.

As an example of how stress can affect your day, fill a mug with tea or coffee, and hold it for one minute. Feel the strain on the ligaments and muscles in your hand and arm. Now imagine holding the mug for five minutes, an hour, or for all day. By 5:00 p.m., your whole body would feel stressed—shoulders lifted up to your ears, the neck crackles or crunches when turned, and you may have symptoms of the beginning of a nasty headache.

We begin our workday with an *empty cup.* Unlike a cup of coffee or tea, in which the weight of the cup decreases with each sip, too much stress can fill our cup to the brim unless we find a way to put a lid on it.

One day I arrived at work and, as usual, checked my e-mail for messages and found one from Ann, my co-worker. "Linda, I have an emergency to attend to. I'll see you at noon." I looked at the stack of projects on my desk and then glanced at the calendar: *9:00—staff meeting; 10:00—train new volunteer.* My cup went from empty to half-full faster than I could reply to the e-mail.

At 9:05 I grabbed the calendar, and while racing to the staff meeting in Pastor's office, I mumbled, "There's no way I'll get my work done by noon without Ann's help." Stress filled the rest of my cup.

When I returned to my office after the meeting, my eyes caught the words in a frame on my wall:

Thank you, Lord, for reminding me to breathe deeply before declaring the day a disaster,

> **Breathe**
> breathe
> breathe

Loving Your Enemies

*I'm telling you to love your enemies. Let them bring
out the best in you, not the worst.* Matthew 5:44

Years ago, I was commissioned as a Stephen Minister, a Christian
caregiver who provides one-to-one care to hurting people in
congregations. After fifty hours of intensive training, I received my
first care-receiver, a woman in her late sixties. She had experienced a
late-life divorce and was concerned about her two sons. My job was to
give her spiritual support.

The first visit in her apartment went well. She shared deeply from
the pain in her heart. I listened and sensed she would be open to prayer.
Before I left, we held hands and prayed together. The next visit went
similarly, except she stopped in the middle of a sentence, leaned closely
to me, and said, "Someone's spying on me . . . my house has been
bugged," and looked at the ceiling above the patio door.

I continued visiting her once a week, until one Sunday after church
when I hung around until she was alone and then said, "Hello, how
are your sons doing?" Her eyes turned from a soft shade of green to
ones that resembled an evil-looking cat's-eye that I remembered from
my brother's marble collection.

She pursed her lips and stared at me for a moment and said, "You
have no business asking me about my sons."

A moment later, I cornered the pastor who knew my assignment,
and announced, "I'm done. She's more than I can handle." I really
wanted to say, "I think she's more than I can love."

*Dear God, help me be more like Jesus when
working with people who are hard to love,*

Pootlagootie

These very tasks, as I go about completing them,
confirm that the Father, in fact, sent me. John 5:34

As a kid, my Norwegian mother referred to me as a pootlagootie (phonetically spelled). Perhaps she was referring to when I'd start dusting the living room furniture, find a pair of my shoes and, while putting them in my closet, decide to make the bed, and a half hour later get back to the living room to finish the dusting.

Some of my habits are hard to break. As the computer booted up I told myself, "I'll start the newsletter, but first, I'll check to see if Pastor Len left an e-mail message over the weekend." No message, but the chair of the finance committee asked if I would check on the supply of window envelopes for the mailing scheduled later in the week. I found a half-empty box and called the supplier to place an order. "We can deliver them tomorrow, without the return address printed." I spent the next fifteen minutes tinkering with the duplicator to figure out how to print the return address on an envelope.

Back in my office, I spotted on my desk a birthday card that needed to be posted and mailed, but the postage machine displayed: INK LOW, and it took a few attempts to get the black box in right side up and the envelope posted.

A moment later, two phone lines began to ring at the same time. I put the first caller on hold and answered the line that unlocked the security door for a member who needed a simple change to a report before his meeting. I pulled up the file, made the correction, and as it came off the printer, the phone rang again. "Hello, you put me on hold and never came back!"

Dear Lord, help me to remember that multitasking
isn't as effective as sticking to a plan,

Volunteer Gems

No one is to show up in the Presence of God empty-handed; each man must bring as much as he can manage, giving generously in response to the blessings of God, your God. Deuteronomy 16:17

The average age of the members in the church I work for is 82. There are a few members under age 60. I consider the youngsters to be in Junior High. I've tagged folks 60-69 as freshman; 70-79, sophomores; 80-89, juniors, 90 to 99, seniors, and for all who have reached 100 years of age, they are true Masters.

The church relies heavily on volunteers, which makes it possible for me to work only four mornings a week (great hours for a semi-retired church secretary and writer). Volunteers answer phones, collate bulletins, do some data entry, or whatever else they *choose* to do. They weave their other activities (playing bridge, golfing, bowling, exercising, etc.) into their commitment to the church office.

June, a junior, is an excellent communicator. She recently fell, broke a hip, and moved into an assisted-living facility where she could receive rehabilitation. June could no longer get to the church, but volunteered to become the new phone coordinator for those needing a ride to church in our bus. Sometimes during her chats with members, she identifies a special need and relays the information to the church office. This important ministry helps June stay in the loop with the office, and the ringing of the phone breaks the silence in her little apartment.

I like to tease volunteers who request time off, "Sure, I'll let you go, but I'll have to dock your pay!" If they work overtime, I say, "You'll see double pay in your next paycheck." They show up as faithfully as the sun rises—we need them, and they need us. Plus, the benefits are heavenly.

*Lord, we give thanks for all who hear the
call to volunteer in the church office,*

Take Hold by the Smooth Handle

The signposts of God are clear and point out the right road. Psalm 19:7

"Always take hold of things by the smooth handle."
—Thomas Jefferson

I believe Jefferson meant when something isn't going as well as anticipated, the path of least resistance should be taken to get through it. While working for the church, I've always felt it is an advantage I have over office workers in the secular world. I can freely witness to my faith and talk to God, without worrying about what anyone else thinks. Hugs are freely available, and tears are accepted without any questions asked. Laughs are plentiful.

Most of the time, the church office is a congenial place to work. However, there are times when God's children are not very lovable, and that includes me.

My son was married in the church where I worked. When I went back to work the following Monday, I was *out of sorts*, as my Grandma used to say. I was tired from out-of-town guests, late nights, and a poor diet. No matter how hard I tried, I couldn't shake loose the nasty spirit that permeated throughout my office. I struggled through my tasks and whined about having to meet with another bride and groom, which I usually enjoyed. During the Wednesday after-school program, the sound of kids running through the hallways seemed louder than usual, and I slammed shut my office door. Friday could not come soon enough to suit me.

Perhaps the path of least resistance should have been in the planning—taking a couple of days off after the wedding to rest and to relish the joy of the weekend.

*Dear God, nudge me and remind me that every now
and then I deserve a day off to pamper myself,*

Thirty Winks at Three

A little nap will lift my spirits. Job 7:13

In many countries businesses shut down after lunch, and everyone takes a nap. It's well known that while Presidents Reagan and Clinton were in office, they handled their stressful days with a thirty-minute power nap at mid-afternoon. My days aren't as stressful as a president's, but when I'm not working, I take short naps whenever possible.

Matthew Walker, an assistant professor of psychology at UC Berkeley, was the lead investigator of a study done on how napping affects the function of the brain. He wrote, "It's as though the e-mail in-box in your hippocampus is full and, until you sleep and clear out those fact e-mails, you're not going to receive any more mail. It's just going to bounce until you sleep and move it into another folder."

I think someone should create an organization called *Naps to Boost the Brain* (NBB), with the slogan, "Bring your nap sack to work for a power nap." Unfortunately, it's not acceptable or practical to take a nap in the church office.

If you are gifted with the ability to take a power nap, I recommend you grab one during your lunch break. If not, go for a *nano nap*. Close your eyes, breathe deeply, and meditate on something pleasant—strolling through a green meadow by a quiet brook or wiggling your toes in the sands of your favorite beach. Repeat as needed.

Dear Lord, thank you for refreshing naps.
I'll be back in thirty minutes,

"Donuts. Is there anything they can't do?"
Matt Groening (cartoonist and creator of *The Simpsons*)

Nature's Way

The health of the apple tells the health of the tree. Luke 6:43

My favorite stories about Jesus are the ones in which he performs miraculous healings of people. I am interested in how my body works and am a big fan of Dr. Oz! He doesn't perform miracles, but he gives his listeners good information about how to stay healthy.

The human body was created to heal itself. Unfortunately, people want a quick miracle cure of a prescribed drug. Pharmacists need computer systems that link all over the world to track the drugs patients are taking to avoid harmful interactions. Some drugs come with a list of side effects that are scarier than the illness itself.

As a joke for my 50th birthday, my husband gave me a twenty-eight day pillbox. A few years ago, I began to use it for one prescription pill and a supplement I take for good bone health, a baby aspirin for my heart and a blood-clotting factor, and two vegetable and two fruit capsules to help my cells do their job.

I'm approaching my Medicare year and am in good health. I have energy to work four mornings a week, write for two to three hours every afternoon, lead retreats, do speaking engagements, work out at the gym three days a week, and promote good health to others as a distributor of Juice Plus+®.

I wonder how it makes God feel when his people neglect their bodies.

Thank you, God, for my body.
Help me stay healthy to glorify you,

This Is a Test

All you need to remember is that God will never let you down;
he'll never let you be pushed past your limit; he'll always be there
to help you come through it. 1 Corinthians 10:13

"Take out a pencil and a sheet of paper." A *pop quiz*—the most dreaded words I could hear while in high school. We don't have pop quizzes on the job but one way or another, we are tested every day.

One Wednesday afternoon, my computer died just as I was completing the bulletin. I went to a spare computer in the office and struggled with an uncomfortable chair, an ergonomic keyboard, and an old mouse that rolled on a little ball instead of an infrared signal. I gave up, stuffed the bulletin into my workbag, and took it home to finish on my faithful laptop.

After getting the bulletin completed, I sent it to my office as an attachment to an e-mail. The next morning I opened the e-mail and downloaded the document, as I had many times before. I quickly printed the document, hit "Save," and handed the bulletin to Ann to be proofread. She found a misspelled name and an omission on the calendar. I went back to the foreign computer to make the corrections and found nothing—*bulletin 09070* had disappeared. Knowing the volunteer would be in any moment to copy the bulletin, I frantically explored through "Recent Places," performed a search on the title and date, and still found no bulletin.

Ann could see that I had been tested enough. She said, "Didn't you tell me that you e-mailed the bulletin to yourself? Download it again and make the corrections."

I thought, *Why didn't I think of that?* The next time I downloaded a bulletin from an e-mail, I remembered to save it in a safe place—the bulletin folder.

Lord, we learn by mistakes, but I'd prefer to have someone
else make them for me when I'm trying to get my work done,

Perfectly Aligned

Think in harmony. Be agreeable. Do all that, and the God of
love and peace will be with you for sure. 2 Corinthians 13:11

While confined to a hospital bed, I received a call from one of the partners of the law firm where I worked. "Linda, where's the ledger that shows the escrow accounts?" I gave my morphine pump another squeeze and thought for a moment before telling him where he could find it.

Besides not knowing where the different account ledgers were, my bosses didn't know what their employees were doing (including the antics of a rookie who thought he was a partner), and what the total caseload looked like. That office messed with the alignment of every part of my being, and I found balance when I went back to work in the church office.

Working in the church does not guarantee crazy-free days or dysfunctional supervisors. Personal problems, lack of training, misfit positions, the bad economy, etc., can affect the alignment of any office.

When the front end of my car needs an alignment, I schedule an appointment and take it to a mechanic. However, when a staff needs to be re-aligned, it may take more than what can be accomplished in a forty-five-minute staff meeting twice a month.

Does your church office need a front-end alignment? Is it time to rearrange desks, get new equipment, or to review each staff member to make sure they are performing their job to the best of their ability?

My attorney bosses eventually dissolved the partnership. They individually aligned their strengths as lawyers and became more financially successful and happier at work and at home.

Lord, help us to discover when it's time to make a change
before everyone in the whole office needs an alignment,

Office Ten Commandments, Plus One

The person who knows my commandments and keeps them,
that's who loves me. John 14:21

1. Honor your boss and your supervisor. (Remember, they aren't God.)
2. You shall not take the name of the Lord in vain or use any profanity. (Does that include *gawd, shoot, and shucky darn?*)
3. Keep the Sabbath Day holy. (You pick the day.)
4. You shall not argue with anyone who thinks they are right—not on the telephone, through e-mail, or by a nasty glare (even when they *are* wrong).
5. You shall not kill the contents of a bulletin, newsletter, and especially the membership database. (Note: "junk in; junk out.")
6. You shall back up your computer files as often as you feel necessary. (Rule of thumb: Back up anything you do not want to restore manually.)
7. You shall not steal. (That includes paper clips, sticky notes, copies, or time.)
8. You shall not covet anything that belongs to your co-worker (desk, plants, lunch, or salary).
9. You shall not gossip about your co-worker (or about any colorful member of the congregation).
10. You shall take appropriate breaks and eat lunch (but not at your desk).
11. You shall love everyone who walks through the door (as God loves you)!

Dear Lord, if we followed your original ten commandments,
we wouldn't need any more rules. Forgive us,

To Be a Model

Friend, don't go along with evil. Model the good. 3 John 1:11

I had grown to my full height (five-feet-ten-inches) by the time I entered high school. During my fast-growing years, I kept trim, and occasionally someone would say, "You should be a model." I never saw myself as thin enough or glamorous enough to be a model, and my three brothers didn't lead me to believe that I'd ever be a contestant in a beauty pageant. Instead, six-on-six girls' basketball became my passion, and instead of my long legs strolling down a runway, they were well used when going in for a lay-up on the basketball court.

After years of working in many capacities in the church office, I realized I had finally become a model: A model citizen (keeping the law), a model worker (showing up and doing what was asked of me), and a model child of God (going to church, teaching Sunday school, singing in the church choir, etc.).

On the job, we have many opportunities to model as Jesus did throughout his life to co-workers, members of the congregation, to a boss, or delivery person. Consider how modeling the following practices in your office could make a difference in your church:

- *Inspire* others to catch their vision, not just your own.
- *Challenge* those who are falling behind in technology to learn how to work smarter, not harder.
- *Enable* others by becoming a cheerleader, coach, or talent scout.
- *Encourage* the office staff to grow spiritually by planning a retreat or attending a seminar every year.

God, thank you for giving us Jesus to model how
we should work and live among each other,

Too Good to Be True

*It's true that God is all-powerful, but he doesn't
bully innocent people.* Job 36:5

If a bargain sounds too good to be true, it probably is. Anyone in the position of purchasing supplies for the office has more than likely been falsely convinced or deceived at least one time by a clever salesman.

We look for bargains when purchasing big items such as cases of paper, because we have little wiggle room in the budget and know that contributions from members pay for office expenses, including our salary.

When I started my new job, I took inventory of the storage closet and cupboards. I'd be doing the purchasing and needed to get a feeling for what had been the purchasing pattern in the past. When I got to a cupboard congested with a stack of fax machine cartridges (that cost about $15 each), I wondered if this office had never heard of the "one in the machine and one on the shelf" rule for supplies that can be obtained within twenty-four hours or less.

The story behind the purchase: A website promised a special offer—buy now and save shipping and handling costs. *The rest of the story*: The first shipment came, and then every month another cartridge arrived until the contract ran out and cartridges overran the cupboard. *Resolution*: None. The confusing language in the contract ("subsequent regular shipments") had been written in a font so small that one with 20/20 vision would need a magnifying glass to read. Unfortunately, the contract was binding. *The good news*: The fax machine never ran out of a cartridge before it passed on to the office-equipment graveyard.

*Dear Lord, help us to learn from our mistakes and to know
that in your eyes, they are only valuable learning experiences,*

The Privilege of Projects

*I've found the recipe for being happy whether full or hungry,
hands full or hands empty.* Philippians 4:12

Ann brought me the new-member forms and asked if I could put the information into the church database. I shot her *my hands are full—I can't believe you are asking me to do one more thing* look and said, "If you don't need it this week, I can do it after I get the newsletter out." Grabbing the folder, I expelled a sigh that sounded like *o-v-e-r-w-h-e-l-m-e-d* and that could have been heard in the pastor's office next door.

Ann couldn't have seen my in-box that led to my frustration, because it was buried under a stack of projects I'd been trying to get to for a week. After she left my office, I looked at the folders and saw *work,* instead of my usual attitude of my tasks being an opportunity to solve a situation or to learn something new while serving God.

A few minutes later I heard a report on National Public Radio: "The unemployment rate increased one percent this past week." Immediately, I felt an avalanche-style attitude adjustment turn the stack of files and the to-do list into opportunities and job security, for a while at least.

The words *job security* are not on the lips of the unemployed. Their in-box overflows with circled newspaper ads, application forms, rejection letters, and stubs from unemployment checks that will eventually stop cluttering their in-box.

*Dear Lord, remind me that if I don't want my job, there are
hundreds of people who'd submit a resume to replace me,*

Senior Power

You shall love your neighbor as yourself. Matthew 22:39

The best part of my job at the all-senior congregation is in the relationships I've developed among my co-workers and the members. Everyone's happy to be part of the staff and congregation, and when everyone's happy, everything runs more smoothly.

Many of the seniors are alone and lonely. Often when a senior is on the fringe of needing care, they become the caregiver for their spouse, or for a neighbor or friend. Some seniors have serious health concerns and have no family in the area to help them make decisions about health care. The church then becomes their family.

One of the youngest members of the church, who makes several trips to the church each week to help with events and activities, recently tripped over her rambunctious little dogs and broke her ankle. Her first reaction was to call the church. Cindy left her desk and went to her home, helped her off the floor, and stayed with her until she had been seen at the emergency room.

For days after the incident, the phone rang at the office with church members offering to drive her to the doctor, take special vegetarian meals to her home, and check on her to make sure she was getting everything she needed. Kate got a long rest from her activities at the church. Who knows, that might have been a God-thing, too.

To no one's surprise, the weekly events moved along with someone picking up extra duty, and Kate now has willing and trained volunteers to give her a good break now and then.

Dear God, we give thanks for willing hands and good feet,

New Tricks of the Trade

We're newcomers at this, with a lot to learn,
and not too long to learn it. Job 8:9

"How far you go in life depends on you being tender with the young, compassionate with the aged, sympathetic with the striving and tolerant of the weak and the strong. Because some day in life you will have been all of these."—George Washington Carver

When I ran across this quote, I thought maybe I should frame it for the wall in the office. Until I retired and picked up a part-time job, I had always been younger than my boss.

The last time I had produced worship booklets on a weekly basis, word processing was still cumbersome. It was more work than worth to scan, cut, and insert hymns or pictures directly into the document.

One day my pastor boss noticed me laboring over a formatting issue. He leaned over my back and said, "Another way to change the tabs is to use your cursor to move the little symbols that look like a baseball home plate to where you want the tab." Then he showed me how to set the right-justified tab and the margins to gain an extra line.

"You are amazing, Pastor Len," I said. "Thanks—and how did you learn all these tricks?"

"By the seat of my pants," he said with a grin. He'd been part of a new church start-up and had served as the pastor/church secretary/janitor, etc. for several years. "You learn how to get things done efficiently!"

Twice blessed, I thought. *A boss who can process words and preach!*
Lord, give all your children the desire to learn
and grow until they take their last breath,

Rules

I post your road signs at every curve and corner. Psalm 119:30

A sign on a church bulletin board said, "Looking for a sign from God? This is it!" If the sign you're looking for is a sea of cars parting so you can get into the carpool lane, you may have a long and disappointing commute!

What kind of signs do you look for from God? I keep my eyes open for a spiritual jolt, such as after praying for a friend who is going through a rough time and then a hummingbird flitters around me. Is that God . . . or odd? Alternatively, when I hear a word on the radio or TV the exact moment I'm reading it in a book or newspaper, I wonder, *Are these signs or coincidences?*

In the church, we have rules that keep our children safe in the nursery, rules that protect pastors and other church workers from situations that can challenge their integrity, rules on how to set up the altar for worship. In the office we have mostly unwritten rules: Let me know when you're going to be away from your desk for more than a few minutes; the next-to-the-last rule to inform the buyer when supplies are running low; and the one about limiting personal phone conversations to emergencies or quick messages. However, my favorite one: No eating bananas in the office.

A few rules found in the Bible good for on the job:

1. Don't let hatred reside in your heart. (John 15:21)
2. Worry about things you *can* change. (Philippians 4:6)
3. Live the revised *K.I.S.S.* principle—keep it simple and straightforward. (1 Corinthians 7:29)
4. Give more of yourself and from your wealth. (Luke 6:37)
5. Expect less—from people and material items. Enjoy what you have. (Mark 10:32)

Lord, let us be grateful for all your rules,

Target Date

*Everything was sorted and piled in mounds. They started doing this in
the third month and didn't finish until the seventh month.*

2 Chronicles 31:7

I missed a newsletter deadline and caused the proofreader to miss his.
The copy volunteer couldn't come in on the rescheduled date, and I had
to armwrestle the duplicator by myself. Many of the volunteers who
collate the newsletter had set aside Wednesday and weren't available
on Thursday, putting a strain on the crew who had to do double the
work. I sighed with relief as I loaded the trays into my car and hoped
I'd never have another newsletter delay again. But when I got to the
post office, I was told their deadline to receive bulk mail was 2:30. The
clock on the wall said 2:45. "You'll have to bring it back tomorrow"
rang in my ears all the way back to the church!

This scenario hasn't really happened to me. However, it is a
recurring dream I've had since taking over the responsibility for
producing the monthly newsletter.

We need deadlines (I hate this word and prefer *target date* or *TD*)
to keep everyone moving in the same direction toward a finish line.
However, call it a deadline or target date, there are people who are
either unaware of, or have no vested interest in, the complexity of
publishing a twelve-page monthly newsletter. And, these same folks
expect to find a copy of the newsletter in their mailboxes before the
beginning of the month and beat it to the telephone to call the office to
see if their name had accidentally been removed from the label list.

Chill—it's only a target date, and the church won't close its door
if the newsletter is a day late once every few years.

*Thank you, God, for the angels (volunteers and staff members)
who give me a hand when I need it,*

"Snudging"

*That's why I tell stories: to create readiness, to nudge the
people toward receptive insight.* Matthew 13:13

Music plays such a big role in worship services, but I had no idea
that music actually affects more than our mood. Music is said to
help align our cells and has a positive impact on creativity, memory,
concentration. It helps us relax and feel more in tune (intended pun)
with our bodies. Current research about music and the body is hoping
to find that music may be useful in combating illness—and without
costly prescriptions!

Since reading the article about music, I realize that it isn't a
coincidence that sometimes I feel the need to play classical music,
usually when I'm under stress—a nudge from God!

God nudges me when I need an attitude adjustment or when I'm
under too much pressure—self-imposed or as part of my work. I call
these nudges *snudges*, because for years I tried to snub God's nudges.
Do you . . .

- Sigh after completing a task or hanging up the receiver after
  a phone conversation?
- Stare at your desk and wonder what to do next?
- Shuffle papers around and are not able to collate thoughts?
- Snap at your co-workers, kids, spouse, friends?
- Sleep restlessly, or nod off at your desk?
- Solicit prayers for help and forget to thank God for the
  blessings?

Begin to recognize when God is snudging you!

*Lord, when my sinful, human nature keeps me from being
all that you desire for me in my life, please nudge me,*

Worshipping Work

By the seventh day God had finished his work. Genesis 2:2

One Sunday morning after church, I had a chat with Pastor Al about the vacancies in the church staff. (F.Y.I.—I was not looking for a job.) He said the church council was not going to rush into replacing the vacant positions until they could come up with a plan that suits the mission of the church. He concluded our conversation with a statement he once heard: We worship our work, we work at our play, and we play at our worship.

"Hmm," I said. "I need to think about this for a moment."

Many years ago, while I was working as the office manager of a law firm, ulcers chewed through the lining of my stomach. I had missed the stress stop signs my body had been flashing for weeks: twitching eye, cold sores around the mouth, stiff neck, tired all the time.

The office, with its dysfunctional partnership, budget, and staffing problems, gave me the opportunity to play *savior.* I had worked long hours and then I would go home and hear, "What's for dinner, Mom?"

It took three months to recover from surgery to repair my stomach. At a follow-up appointment, my doctor (an internist who grew up in Asia) said, "Americans are too sincere about their job." ·

"Hmm," I said. "I need to think about this a moment." That's when I realized I had been forfeiting my health for a job. Through this new revelation, God performed a miracle in my mind: I don't need to kill myself with unnecessary acts of kindness, always saying yes to everyone, and thinking that if I were not around, the office would close down.

Creator God, help us figure out that when we are too sincere
about our work, there may be consequences,

Happy Thoughts

Your thoughts—how rare, how beautiful!
God, I'll never comprehend them! Psalm 139:17

"Think happy thoughts," my mom said. *How can I think happy thoughts when my whole life is a mess?* I had just walked away from my thirty-nine-year marriage to get my head clear, and from a job I loved.

Mother handled my marital problem in her own way—she listened, but didn't give me any advice, other than "Think happy thoughts." It took me two years, thousands of dollars in therapy, and a greater understanding of myself to realize that she was right. Happy thoughts make for a happier person—and marriage.

There are days when I find it hard to find one thing I like about my job. I usually love my job. All it takes to get off on the wrong foot for the day is to walk into the office fifteen minutes late because of an accident or road maintenance.

When I get to my desk, I feel behind, and when feeling behind, I'm not in control. Phone calls begin to *interfere* with my work (and my work is to answer the phone). I have no patience for the UPS delivery man, even though he is always courteous and friendly. On days like this, I need the "joke-for-the-day" that a member of the church e-mails to me, to shake me out of my self-induced bad mood.

My mother is right—when I get into the sinking-in-self-pity mode, I need to think happy thoughts: *I'm going to see my granddaughter after work . . . . I've got a great tuna salad for lunch, plus fresh strawberries . . . . Tomorrow is Friday!*

Dear Father, when thoughts and deeds threaten to
ruin my day, help me to think happy thoughts,

Sunrise, Sunset

God rises on you, his sunrise glory breaks over you.
Isaiah 60:2

When I see one of God's masterpieces in the sky, I often find myself humming the tune *Sunrise, Sunset*, from *Fiddler on the Roof*. God uses man-made pollution and dust stirred up in the Arizona desert to swirl shades of magenta, goldenrod, and turquoise around in the sky to create an art gallery that fades away in a few minutes.

At home, I can't see the glorious sunrises and sunsets, unless I go out my front door and stand in the middle of the street. Most of the time I'm too preoccupied or in too much of a hurry to stop and catch the amazing color shows.

As the sun sets on your workday, think about how you have made a difference today to someone who needed comfort or inspiration. Perhaps it was as simple as the phone call you handled to help a single mom find a food bank or a family new in the area looking for a church close to their home.

As a church employee, your "work blessings" will not make the evening news, but God's watching and knows that your contributions to all kinds of ministry in your office make their own gallery of goodness.

Ministry can tax your energy, even on a good day. When you leave your office worn out and need to muster up energy to drive home, try this quick method to help you relax: Place one hand on your belly and the other on your chest. Breathe in slowly until your lungs expand to the top of your ribcage; slowly breathe out. Shake your hands! Gently twist your neck from side to side, roll your eyes, stick out your tongue, and then scrunch your facial muscles. Now don't you feel better?

Dear Lord, be the breath in our bodies when we are tired,

Trusting

Trust God from the bottom of your heart; don't try to figure out everything on your own. Proverbs 3:5

Theodore Roosevelt was quoted as saying, "In any moment of decision, the best thing you can do is the right thing, the next best thing is the wrong thing, and the worst thing you can do is nothing." I wondered, *How many times have I made the right decision that in the end wasn't so great?* The biggest decision I make these days in the office is whether to buy pens with blue ink or black ink.

Shortly after starting a new job, I snooped around the storeroom and found boxes of overhead projector sheets, rolodex cards (large and small), and a lifetime supply of yellow legal pads. According to the dust on the overhead projector, it hadn't seen daylight in years. Rolodex cards have given way to the ease of using a database, and note taking is done on laptops or digital recorders. I wondered what nonprofit organization might be able to use this stuff—perhaps in a third-world country such as Haiti.

In another room, I looked into a cupboard and found cartons of wax ink cubes for the color laser printer. After a quick mental calculating, there was about a five-year supply—we could only hope the printer would last that long. A slick, online supplier had sold the church a great deal, which included a surprise shipment every three months—whether we needed it or not. After many telephone conversations with customer service and a firm letter from the pastor, the company agreed to let us return the ink.

We learn by making decisions, and then we learn again from the bad decisions. Sometimes we make mistakes because we are too trusting that no one would take advantage of a church.

Lord, help us when we need to make decisions
that affect the church-office budget,

In a Rut

Make the road straight and smooth, a highway fit for our God. Fill in the valleys, level off the hills, smooth out the ruts, clear out the rocks. Isaiah 40:3

Growing up in Iowa, I lived on a gravel road. My brothers and I boarded a "yellowhound" bus every morning at 7:00 for the hour-long ride to school. First one on—first one off—saved us from being on the bumpy roads for more than a little over an hour each day. Every spring the roads thawed from months of freezing weather and took on the appearance of an old scrub board, like the one my mother used to scrub the knees of my three brothers' trousers.

In my life experiences, I have found that a rut in the road is an opportunity for me to stumble and then get up and continue with the rest of my journey. The ruts in my life have changed since I became a city girl. There are plenty of bad roads from hard use, but I can avoid the ones I don't need to travel.

On the job I get into a rut now and then, too. Sometimes doing the same project week after week becomes all work and no fun.

Norman Vincent Peale, author of *The Power of Positive Thinking*, suggested three ways to break out of a dull routine:

Change your pace.
Seek the zest in life.
Forget yourself.

I try to remember that what I do in the office is not about me, but it's about my call to serve God. If I get bored, or in a rut, it's time for me to have a chat with the creator.

Lord, help turn a rut in my workday into a smooth path
for those who walk with me on my journey,

Nurturing Relationships

Cultivate your own relationship with God, but don't impose it on others. Romans 14:22

"Notice throughout the week relationships that cross your path, decisions you have to make, challenges you have to face, empty tasks that drain you, and opportunities that fill you up! Watch others. Reflect on the disappointments and surprises that come up in the regular course of the week. Each can nurture your thinking about what you really value."—John Blumberg

Mr. Blumberg must have hovered around a *perfect* office during a *perfect* week to come up with this quote.

Wouldn't it be great while working in the church office if we could take time to notice the connections being made between staff members, and/or with lay leaders, pastors, or the members of the congregation, and to be a part of these new relationships?

I'd love to be able to make decisions that pop up while I'm in the middle of a challenge to figure out why the network isn't working, or why the altar flowers weren't delivered for the Sunday service.

I do pray that God won't turn surprises into a disappointment during any part of the week while I'm preparing a worship booklet or getting ready for a new-member orientation. On Fridays while I'm tidying up my desk, I'd like to review my week and think about how every event nurtured my thinking about what I really value about my job—more than the paycheck.

Weeks aren't like this in most offices, Mr. Blumberg, but you've given office workers something to dream about.

*Dear God, when I complain about my job, you know
I just need to take a break and nurture my relationship
with you and those I work with in the office,*

Making Christmas Memories

They left, running, and found Mary and Joseph, and the
baby lying in the manger. Luke 2:16

As our children got older, it became harder for any of us to get motivated to make the journey to Iowa to celebrate Christmas with the grandparents. After one Christmas when the weather had interrupted our nice drive to Iowa, and I had been crabby from preparing 3,000 worship booklets for five worship services on Christmas Eve, I had a conversation with my husband and kids. "Next year, do we go to Grandma's house for Christmas or stay home and play with the new toys?" Even the big kid (Glen) voted to stay home.

Our first Christmas Eve alone in our own home gave us the opportunity to plan how we wanted to celebrate. We began by going to a children-friendly service held later in the afternoon and then went home to the fragrance of homemade chicken noodle soup warming in the Crock-Pot, which I made a day earlier. After supper, we had our first Christmas pre-present-opening service. Each of our children had been put on alert earlier in the week that they would have to participate in the service by singing a song, reciting a poem, or reading a classic Christmas story *before* any of the packages were opened.

We nibbled on cookies, drank hot cocoa, and applauded the children's presentations. The moment my son read the words, *and to all a good night*, the littlest pair of hands distributed the Christmas presents.

Now that I'm a grandparent, I'd never suggest that you boycott ever going to visit grandparents for Christmas! If you will be away from your home over the holidays, pick a day before leaving and celebrate the birth of Jesus as a family. Create some memories of a peaceful Christmas celebration in your home.

Dear Lord, help us to find peace, love, and joy this Christmas,

Take Out Your Pencil

Thus the priest will make atonement for him for his error.
Leviticus 5:18

Years ago, before the luxury of scanning and editing music directly into the pages of worship booklets, I'd have to photocopy the music, cut out only the melody lines and the lyrics to be sung (to conform to copyright rules), and then paste the strips of paper onto graph paper. The song would then be taped into the pre-calculated space in the booklet. After copying the bulletin, I'd pull the pasted-up songs out of the bulletin and file them for future use.

One Sunday morning as Pastor Jerry gave the announcements, he said, "While I'm telling you about the events coming up this week, please take out a pencil, so we can make an adjustment to the worship booklet."

Immediately, my ears perked up, and I wondered, *Now what did I do?* Finally, Pastor said, "Now, at the hymn on page three, starting at verse two, draw an arrow to verse four and then another one from verse four to verse two."

Apparently, the song hadn't worked well during the Saturday evening service when they sang:

Verse 1. *O blessed spring . . .*
Verse 2. *As when winter comes . . .*
Verse 3. *When autumn cools . . .*
Verse 4. *Through summer heat . . .*

Upon arriving to work the next morning, the first thing I did was to pull apart the poorly pasted-up song and put the seasons back in the order that God had created them.

Pastor Jerry never mentioned the incident to me. He could tell by the deep blush of my cheeks as I had sat in the pew that I had caught my error.

Lord, bless the grace-filled pastors and supervisors
that use creative ways to cover my errors,

Signs to Hang Around the Office

So if they don't trust you and aren't convinced by the first sign, the second sign should do it. Exodus 4:8

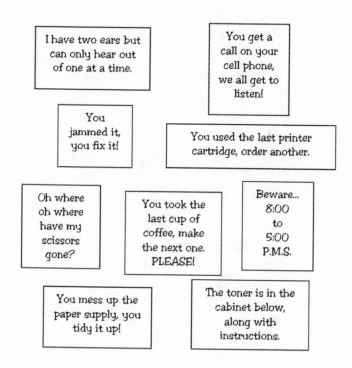

I have two ears but can only hear out of one at a time.

You get a call on your cell phone, we all get to listen!

You jammed it, you fix it!

You used the last printer cartridge, order another.

Oh where oh where have my scissors gone?

You took the last cup of coffee, make the next one. PLEASE!

Beware...
8:00
to
5:00
P.M.S.

You mess up the paper supply, you tidy it up!

The toner is in the cabinet below, along with instructions.

No, I don't have these signs hanging around my office, but there are days when I wish I could be so forward as to tell people I work with what I need from them: cooperation, courtesy, and consideration for those who use the same space and equipment.

Perhaps there is a better way of conveying the messages in these signs without being so obvious!

Dear Lord, help us learn to be a good co-worker or companion and to appreciate learning experiences around the office,

Cleanliness in the Eye
of the Beholder

Clean up your act—the way you live, the things you do—so
I can make my home with you in this place. Jeremiah 7:3

We have a new maintenance man at our church. The former one had been around for a number of years and had become curmudgeon-like. He insisted we communicate by e-mail so not to have a face-to-face conversation. Our new maintenance man doesn't even have e-mail. He also doesn't have the experience the former person had, and we (the office staff) are now in the process of "training" him.

I have come to realize that even though I am the queen of cleaning in my own home, there is a big difference between house cleaning and church cleaning. My cleaning kit includes Q-tips and a one-half inch paintbrush, several dimensions and types of cleaning rags, plus at least a dozen different cleaning products. The maintenance man has a bottle of smelly orange cleaning solution, window cleaner, a supply of red cleaning rags, paper towels, a mop large enough to cover a two-foot swipe in one stretch, and a vacuum cleaner, without the cute little attachments that you can rip off the holder to catch a stray cobweb or get in the corner under my desk.

"Just how clean does a church building need to be?" I asked myself. Well, when it comes to the women's room, it must pass the white-glove test, or I'll be the one to have to tell the maintenance man on Monday morning to "try to do a little better job cleaning around the faucet; buff it while you're at it."

Dear Lord, help me mind my own business,

Flowers Galore to God's Glory

No need to panic over alarms or surprises, or predictions that doomsday's just around the corner, because God will be right there with you; he'll keep you safe and sound. Proverbs 3:25

It was a Saturday evening around 5 p.m., and I stopped by the church to see if the maintenance man had reset the fellowship hall for the next day. As I walked through the hallway, I noticed that there were no altar flowers on the table where the deliveryman left them every Saturday afternoon. I remembered ordering two bouquets for donors, who were very specific about why they wanted the flowers for this particular Sunday. After searching every possible hiding place to find a couple of two-foot tall floral arrangements, I found no flowers. *They've forgotten the flowers again!* I thought (which happened a few weeks earlier).

I called the floral company and got a recording, "... office closed." On my way home, I drove to a local grocery store and purchased two of the largest bouquets available, for a cost of $67.00. Ouch! However, I felt grateful that the folks who donated the flowers would not be disappointed with my choices.

The next morning I arrived early at church, balancing a bouquet in each hand. The first thing I saw was two huge bouquets flanking each side of the communion table. I almost dropped the flowers! Perhaps I had panicked in vain, but I'm not fond of explaining why someone's flowers weren't available for their anniversary celebration or in memory of their wife or husband.

Early the next week I called the florist and learned that deliveries are made up to 7:00 p.m. on Saturdays. *Now I know,* I thought. *I hope someone enjoyed the extra flowers.*

Dear God, I'm not sure you care about altar flowers,
but I care about your children and want to make them happy,

Happitude

Laugh with your happy friends when they're happy. Romans 12:14

Jenny had a natural smile that not even Botox injections could improve. If I didn't know better, I would have thought she added something more than hazelnut flavored Coffee-mate® to her cup of java each morning. There were days when I'd use the back hallway to avoid having to muster up a smile to greet her first thing in the morning.

I consider myself a morning person, but I never had a Jenny in my household. I like being the first one up in the morning and enjoy a cup of tea on the patio where I can do my morning meditations and talk to God.

It seems as if my workday goes better if I'm the first one to arrive at the office. I peruse the bulletin boards on the way to my desk for outdated material, check the answering machine for messages, and then sit down at my computer to catch up on my e-mails. I've done this routine for years, and it grounds me for the day.

Occasionally, I'd miss my morning time with God. On those mornings, when Jenny greeted me with her "happitude" smile and eyes that flashed the "Ain't Life Great?" sign, I'd want to go into hibernation.

I recognized it was my attitude that kept me from allowing Jenny's happitude to rub off on me first thing in the morning. By break time, I was finally able to accept and return her happitude.

Dear Lord, I can't be all to everyone first thing in the morning without beginning my day with quiet time with you,

God in Every Direction

The signposts of God are clear
and point out the right road. Psalm 19:8

"Look back and thank God.
Look forward and trust God.
Look around and serve God.
Look within and find God!"

As a farm girl from Iowa I learned the global directions as part of daily living—"I'll be in the north field until noon" or "Go half a mile south and turn right and you'll find the schoolhouse." However, since I moved into Sun City, the sun has come up in the north. I'm 90 degrees off most of the time when I try to figure out where I am. Perhaps it is because the first time I came to Sun City, I flew in to visit my parents and the airplane must have made a 90-degree turn around the airport before landing.

I'm grateful for my G.P.S., but a bit embarrassed that I have to use it to find my way around my own neighborhood.

In our work and in our relationships we need to figure out where we are and then how we can make things right. We can look back and see how we've created challenging situations. We can look forward to better days, opportunities to change. We can look around and see where we can make a difference in someone else's day, and we can look within for satisfaction.

In my relationship with God, I don't have to worry about which direction to seek him, and better yet, I'm never lost!

Dear God, thank you for your global
positioning at all times,

"We had an intervention the other day at lunch.
Someone tried to eat a doughnut."
—Michael Woods

Who Are You?

Lucky the men and women who work for you, getting to be around
you every day and hear your wise words firsthand!
2 Chronicles 9:5

T F   You stop by someone's desk and offer a hand.

T F   You anticipate when someone needs help.

T F   You encourage others to stay on track.

T F   You get caught up in other people's projects.

T F   You are aware not everyone wants to be helped.

T F   You resent that no one else wants to help you.

T F   You get emotionally drained.

T F   You find it hard to get your own work done.

If you answer True to most of these questions, you are a nurturer (or a mother!).

I have found that volunteers in the office tend to be nurturers. Joyce is my Tuesday volunteer. She spent her whole work career as an elementary schoolteacher. She is punctual, predictable, and precise—a no-nonsense type of a person who says what she thinks. I'm grateful she is a positive thinker! She also tends to mother me a little. When Joyce hears the clinking of the candy-jar lid, I'll hear, "Linda, you don't really want that piece of candy. Get a nice cold glass of water instead."

Some days I don't even realize she is in the office except for when I hear her answer the phone. Other days she seems to have an extra pair of hands and is willing to do just about anything I ask her to do. She always does it with a smile and says, "I'm here to help. I like to keep busy." My job is to make sure I keep Joyce from wearing out and to make sure she will want to come back next week. Nurturing people are not particularly good at taking care of themselves.

Dear Lord, help those who nurture others to
understand that they need to be nurtured, too,

Procrastination Thief

Don't procrastinate—
there's no time to lose. Proverbs 6:40

"Procrastination is attitude's natural assassin. There is nothing
so fatiguing as an uncompleted task."—William James

William James, one of the founders of modern psychology, spoke those words to which I can relate. I used to sew for myself and some for the children. However, before I would think about dragging out my sewing machine to sew a new dress, I'd force myself to do my ironing. I don't mind ironing, but I procrastinate away every opportunity to get caught up. "I'll do it while I'm watching Dr. Oz" or "I don't have enough to bother to get the ironing board out." Therefore, it stacks up. But because an unfinished project frustrates me, I get the ironing done and then enjoy sewing.

At the office I tend to procrastinate over the little projects—data entry of a new address, filing, making sign-up sheets for the event book. Any of these projects would take a minute or two, but it doesn't seem worth my time to stop doing something I really enjoy and get the little stuff done. Unfortunately, the little projects clutter up my desk and in-box, and when I need the information, I can't put my hands on it.

Recently, I read the average person loses fifty-five minutes a day (roughly fourteen days a year) looking for things they know they have but can't find. I can most likely add a few minutes and days to that statement the older I get. And it's a good thing my boss doesn't dock me fifty-five minutes of pay on days that I spend looking for lost items.

Dear God, help me find extra time to
serve you by being more orderly,

Rules for Happier Living

God, mark us with grace and blessing! Smile! Psalm 67:1

It takes more than a paycheck to get me out of my home to face the traffic and my desk with never-ending tasks. I need joy! And a sense of being happy to come back to work the next day. From an article in *Pulpit Helps* (author unknown), here are ten ways to increase the level of happiness in your life:

1. Give something away (no strings attached). This could be as simple as a smile.
2. Do a kindness (and forget it). How about calling someone you haven't seen around the church just to say hello?
3. Spend time with the aged (their experiences are priceless)—if only to spend a few minutes really listening to them.
4. Look intently into the face of a baby (and marvel)—if not a baby, enjoy the antics of animals.
5. Laugh often (life's lubricant)—perhaps at yourself.
6. Give thanks (a thousand times a day is not enough)—thank God and others you work with.
7. Pray (or you will lose the way)—all day long.
8. Work (with vim and vigor)—work is good for the soul.
9. Plan as though you will live forever (you will)—don't leave pebbles on the path that you'll want to recover before they are found by someone else.
10. Live as though you will die tomorrow (because you will die on some tomorrow)—and make amends with everyone.

God blesses us with happiness and is smiling on us—all he wants is for us to smile back.

Lord, happiness completes me. Let me share it around,

Polish Your Halo

But even then an angel could come, a champion—there are
thousands of them!—to take up your cause. Job 33:23

"Women are angels. And when someone breaks
their wings they simply continue to fly . . . on a broomstick.
They are flexible like that." (Source Unknown)

I seriously doubt if anyone believes I am like an angel. My halo is
tarnished, and my wings have been clipped on many occasions. It is
nice to have someone say, "Linda, you've been an angel to me today,"
because some weeks or months, compliments don't happen often
enough to keep the wind moving beneath my wings.

It is the little things that the members of my congregation
appreciate, such as finding a precious earring that was lost in the
third row from the back on the left side of the sanctuary. Sometimes
I think I'm too busy to fly around the church on a broom hunting for
an earring the size of a dime.

Some of my useful angelic lines:

"I know you're worried about your earring. Let me get your phone
number, and I'll call you back in the next fifteen minutes;

"I checked the Lost and Found box yesterday, and there was
nothing new added to it. I'll check with the janitor later today and call
you back tomorrow; or

"Stop by and I'll help you look for the earring."

The big-ticket items, such as making absolutely no errors in the
church bulletin, won't put feathers in your wings. It's the little things
that make your halo shine!

Dear Lord, help me remember that the little things count,

"Well while you're thinking, think me a cup of coffee and a
chocolate donut with some of those little sprinkles on top,
will you?"—U.S. Marshall Marshal Samuel Gerard played
by Tommy Lee Jones in *The Fugitive*

A Friend

God puts spontaneous songs in their hearts. Job 35:10
"A friend is someone who knows your song
and sings it to you when you have forgotten it."
(Source unknown)

My co-worker, Cindy, and I seem to be on the same frequency so often. I'll be thinking about something, and she'll begin to talk about the same subject. But what is even more fun is when someone says something and both of us break out into the same song. I'm only good for the first line, but it breaks up the moment with a little laughter.

It's also good that Cindy can read my mood. She seems to know when I'm stressed out and doesn't hesitate to ask, "Okay, what's going on?" Sometimes it is something going on with one of my adult kids, and because she, too, has an adult child, she takes time to listen and will offer to pray about the situation.

I am privileged to work in an environment where co-workers easily become friends. I spend more daytime hours with my co-workers than with my other friends. Friends in the office know what it's like to be a church employee and check on each other to make sure no one is a little too generous with their time or being taken advantage of by someone like a committee person who never gets the report in on time to copy before their next meeting. A friend will jump in and say, "Let me do this for you so you can finish the newsletter."

I've worked in the secular world, and even though I enjoyed the working relationships I formed, they were not like my faith partners in the office.

*Dear Lord, thank you for putting Cindy in the office
next to mine to help me balance my day,*

A Balancing Act

We can grow up healthy in God only as he nourishes us.
Colossians 2:19

Many factors keep us from staying "healthy" and performing our best on the job. I remember dragging myself home after a long day at the office and being greeted at the back door by three kids and a hungry husband, wishing I could order in Chinese food and a massage therapist. It took years for me, as a type "A" personality, to figure out that I could no longer chair the women's church group, be a scout leader, and play bridge until midnight on a Tuesday evening. After spending the weekend trying to do all the things I did as a stay-at-home mom, I was almost relieved when Monday morning rolled around and I could go back to work!

There are numerous personal-growth articles on the internet about life balancing. Some authors relate life balancing to balancing the wheels on a car. To avoid a life of thudding and being steered in directions you don't want to go, you need to check the "air" in your life wheel.

Try this easy exercise to help determine how well you are balancing all aspects of your life: Draw a circle and divide it into eight equal pieces, like a pie. Label each piece with a title that represents important parts of your life, such as Health, Family/Friends, Romance, Business/Career, Fun/Recreation, Finances, Personal Spiritual Growth, and Physical Environment. In each section of the circle, give yourself a number between 1 (the weakest) and 10 that best indicates how well you see yourself doing in each area of your life. A perfect score would be 80. Fewer than 40 points may indicate a need to divide your pie into less pieces!

We know, Lord, that we can never be perfect in our lives,
but we seek you to help us get into balance,

When to Laugh

A right time to cry and another to laugh. Ecclesiastes 3:3

You may think you've heard of just about everything that can happen in the church office, until you read stories from other church secretaries (sources to remain anonymous to protect their jobs!):

"I do bulletins for two English services and one Spanish service, and we use acronyms for the books that the services come from. The Spanish acronym is LOC, but one time I inadvertently put LOCO."

"I made a typo in the bulletin, and later I learned that it was a long-standing 'joke' that the pastor would say from the pulpit, 'The mistake of the week is . . . .'" [Note from editor: Not funny!]

"I am secretary of the same church where I worship. This year we used a new format for our church directory, so I had to retype all the data. After printing the new directory and distributing it to all the members, it was gently pointed out to me that I had typed in my own phone number incorrectly—a number I've had for 20 years . . . and after proofreading the new directory THREE times!"

"An older male member came in and asked to use my Word program. Someone had told him that if he typed in certain words the Thesaurus would give options. The word he typed came up with sexually explicit alternatives!"

To all who are reading this meditation, please learn to laugh at your own mistakes, instead of crying! I'm sure God is laughing with you.

Dear Lord, thanks for giving us the choice of crying or laughing,

One Body

Listen to me, listen well: Eat only the best,
fill yourself with only the finest. Isaiah 55:2

We were born with our natural immune system already in place. The system is far too complex for me to explain in less than four-hundred words, but I do know, from personal experience, when the immune system fails, we get colds, flu, sore throats, strep throat, ear or sinus infections. And, we miss work! Worse yet, when we try to work through an illness, often we end up getting sicker and spreading the bug to others.

Our body is an amazing fix-it machine. But it needs help from the mechanics—God and the owner of the body. Here are suggestions based on the 2011 government's new nutrition icon (formerly referred to as a food pyramid), *The Food Plate*:

- Fruits and vegetables should occupy half your plate! Your mother was right, "Eat your fruits and vegetables!"
- Fill another quarter of your plate with a low-fat protein to help manufacture white blood cells and to be the building blocks for the cells.
- The last quarter on the plate is for carbohydrates, such as whole grain bread or pasta.

Other ways to help boost your immunity is to switch to tea after a morning cup of coffee, as green tea is an antioxidant, and chamomile tea may boost the immune system. Greek or other "live culture" yogurts help to build up friendly bacteria in the intestines to fight off bad bacteria.

For heart health, get out from behind your desk and take a walk as often as you can, and you'll get a bonus in helping to keep your weight within an acceptable range.

Lord, you gave us an amazing body. Help us to take care
of it by exercising and eating a healthy diet,

Mind Over Matter

*You're blessed when you get your inside world—your
mind and heart—put right.* Matthew 5:8

"I close my eyes, and soon I find I'm in a playground in my mind."
(Paul Vance/Lee Pockriss/Clint Holmes—1973)

One day at work, I spent a half hour cutting little squares from a sheet of paper. By the time I finished the project, I had planned what I'd prepare for dinner, thought about what movie I'd like to pick up at the Red Box, and pictured myself enjoying the evening cuddling on the love seat with my husband. The playground in my mind took over and kept me from getting anxious about a mundane project that a first-grader could have done.

God gave us a mind, not only to use for intelligence, but as a source of play. I discovered how to use the fertile playground in my mind when my children were young, and I cleaned houses for spare income. After months of cleaning the same five-bedroom, two-story mini-mansion (with only two occupants), I realized if I didn't find something to do while looking for dirt to clean, I'd go crazy. I began to think about ways to re-arrange the furniture in my living room, what gifts to buy my children for Christmas, or the perfect way for my husband and I to celebrate our wedding anniversary. Before I realized it, four hours had passed.

Instead of only planning and dreaming while working, try letting your senses play. Image the sound of a waterfall and heat from the sun penetrating your back while lying on a beach. Listen for the sounds of waves slapping at the shore or children laughing while body surfing. Smell the fragrance of the lei around your shoulders. Oh, I did it again! Making plans while I'm writing—this time for a vacation in Hawaii!

*Dear God, the master of all play, thank you for
giving us a playground in the mind,*

Building Blocks

David blessed God in full view of the entire congregation . . .
"You hold strength and power in the palm of your hand to
build up and strengthen all." 1 Chronicles 29:9,11

When my son was a toddler, I'd sit on the floor and show him how to play with the building blocks. I wasn't particularly patient with little kids. To be honest, I'd rather have been scrubbing the floor I was sitting on than stacking little wooden blocks. I'd get the tower built about a foot tall, and a little hand would knock it down. Time after time, I'd rebuild the tower, and time after time, he'd knock it down. Soon I'd scoop up the blocks, put them away, and give him a tractor to play with.

Today I serve as part of a team that provides the building blocks for ministry inside and outside of the church walls. I work with pastors, co-workers, board or committee members, and with the members of the congregation to help create a community of servants to fulfill the ministry of the church.

In individual ways, each of us is called to be a life coach—a person trained to help their students achieve their life goals. This is done by making these students accountable for their action—or lack of action. God—the Life Coach of the Church—gives us opportunities to coach in our homes, with friends, at school, or in business. He sent Jesus to Earth to set an example as to how it should be done, and the Holy Spirit keeps us accountable for our actions.

Now when the building blocks of my faith tumble, I have support to build them up again.

Dear Lord, keep me focused on the building
blocks needed to live a faithful life,

Queen of Multitasking

God of my master Abraham, make things turn out
well in this task I've been given. Genesis 24:42

One of the main differences between men and women is that women are better at multitasking. It's probably a learned behavior from the days when men went out to get the food and the women stayed home to cook the dinner while taking care of children, making sure everyone had clothes to wear, and providing a social life for the family.

Women like to brag about being able to multitask. "I can run the Risograph machine, folding machine, and answer the phone at the same time." Great for the office, but is this great for the worker?

Too much multitasking can be hard on the body and the mind. If one multitasks all day long at the office and then goes home and multitasks the household, too, he or she may become like a spaceship spinning out of control. When concentrating on more than one thing at a time, work turns into a four-letter word.

I challenge you to pick several projects you would normally multitask, and do them separately. Concentrate on the process. Try to find inner peace from completing each task separately. Did doing each project one at a time take enough extra time to warrant the stress you experienced when you did them all at the same time?

Multitasking leads to the possibility of becoming a workaholic. That's a whole other problem!

Dear God, help me to see the beauty in what I do
instead of the work I make of it,

Finding Your Passion
(at work!)

Whatever happened to your passion, your famous mighty
acts, your heartfelt pity, your compassion? Isaiah 63:15

Have you ever gotten so caught up in a project that it seemed like only minutes passed when hours actually slipped by? That's what is called "finding your passion."

A couple of years ago my boss assigned me the responsibility of creating the monthly newsletter. Of all the tasks I've had working in the church, producing a newsletter has never been part of my job description. I had used Microsoft Publisher to make fliers and posters, but had never been challenged to place little boxes all over a blank page, arrange columns, figure out how to insert clip art or pictures within a box, etc. The first newsletter I did by myself took two weeks, working part-time. Over the next few months, the production became easier, and I enjoyed the opportunity to learn something new.

One day Cindy stopped by my desk and said, "Why are you still here? It's three o'clock." I usually go home at noon. I'd gotten caught up in the cloud of project passion and the time escaped me.

I do the same thing when writing my books or preparing for a retreat. The hours fly by, and I reluctantly have to quit to rustle up something for dinner.

God privileges each of us with the gift of passion, but the gift may be too tightly wrapped in busyness to experience. Or, it may be buried beneath feelings of drudgery or the lack of imagination to create new ways to make a project more fun.

If you are not experiencing passion at work, I pray that you have something outside of your workday that gives you that wonderful sense of time escaping out the window.

Dear Lord, help us to find our passion
as we fulfill our call to work in the church,

Senses

Springs of water will burst out in the wilderness, streams
flow in the desert. Hot sands will become a cool oasis,
thirsty ground a splashing fountain. Isaiah 35:6

Stressed out? Think of a place or event that you remembered as being safe, peaceful, restful, beautiful, and happy. Our five senses are God's gift for us to help enjoy life more fully. Natural senses can help muster up a complex image, such as lying on a beach in a deserted cove. Can you see the ocean cliffs and sand around you, hear the waves crashing against rocks, smell the salt in the air, and feel the warmth of the sun and a gentle breeze on your body? Or, if you prefer mountains, can you smell the wild flowers, observe animals grazing, or listen to a waterfall splashing into a stream?

I have a photograph that I took while on vacation in northern Minnesota. I enlarged it, and it hangs in my office where I can see it whenever I enter the room—a reminder of a place I'd rather be!

Over the years, I began to visualize the sailboat moored at the shore as a vessel at rest. The still, shallow water as an invitation to wade and squish sand between my toes—as I did as a child. When I look at the vastness of the blue water and sky, and the jagged line of trees on the other side of the lake, I can almost hear God saying, "This is my handiwork! Enjoy!" While picture-gazing, I began to breathe more fully and feel at peace—at least until the telephone rings.

Dear Lord, thank you for giving us senses to help us relax,

"Are doughnuts the healthiest food you can eat? No.
So why do I say they are good for you? Because they
are a comfort food, relieve stress, and
make you feel good."—Source Unknown

See the Heart

*Don't pick on people, jump on their failures, criticize their faults—
unless, of course, you want the same treatment.* Matthew 7:1

"Every action of our lives touches on some chord that will
vibrate in eternity."—Edwin Hubbel Chapin

She gave me a big hug. I wondered, *What was that all about?* Gloria
usually was a bit tight—almost rude—and demanding. I had only
made copies of a program the moment she asked for them. Later that
day, I thought about the encounter with Gloria. Perhaps no one sees
through her tough, in-your-face attitude.

Stephen R. Covey wrote a successful self-help book called *The Seven
Habits of Highly Effective People.* Habit 5 is "Seek first to understand, then
to be understood." He told about observing a father and his children
riding on the commuter train. The kids were out of control, and the
father just sat there as if he were in a trance. Covey was tired and
getting more and more annoyed with the father, because he didn't seem
to care what his kids were doing. Before he totally blasted the father,
he learned that they had just left the hospital and that the children's
mother had died.

Jesus treated everyone with kindness—firmness when necessary—
but he saw through the shell of people and went straight to their
heart to heal and give them whatever they needed. When we attempt
to understand those we encounter at the office, before jumping to
conclusions, it helps us react in a more caring, respectful, and positive
manner.

Dear God, help us to see your face in everyone we meet,

A Harmonious Habitat

When we worship the right way, God doesn't stir us up into confusion;
he brings us into harmony. 1 Corinthians 14:33

Many large corporations and restaurant owners consult with a feng shui (pronounced "fung schway") specialist to advise them how to design their buildings and offices for success. Feng shui is an ancient approach to the way environment affects us—from how we feel to how we act. Energy is the key and how to make it flow freely by utilizing productive water, wood, metal, fire, and earth—resulting in clarity, peace, joy, and prosperity.

I went to a learning session about feng shui and immediately went home and cleared out everything beneath my bed, which stops the energy flow, but that's as far as I got. One day I surveyed my home office to see what might be confusing the energy flow in the room. A stack of books and magazines on the floor only reminded me how far behind I am in my intentional reading material. That didn't give me a sense of joy. A bookcase jammed full of books drained me even more, so I moved the bookcase to a different room, and that helped me with clarity.

One wall seemed too rigid and confining, so I angled a cabinet in the corner, and immediately the room seemed to flow. It felt good. I tackled the filing overflowing in the basket at the end of my desk, and came to a better understanding of what was going on in my business. (Not much prosperity!) With everything neat, the dust seemed more obvious. After cleaning the room, I wanted to stay in my creative cave and tackle some long-overdue projects.

Without an expert in the field, feng shui is a bit confusing, but we can follow the guidance of an even more powerful consultant—the Holy Spirit—to enjoy the time we spend in our offices.

Dear Lord, let your spirit permeate throughout my office,

In Your Easter Bonnet

Attention, all! See the marvels of God!
He plants flowers and trees all over the earth. Psalm 46:8

How many hats do you wear during your workday? Any person in the workforce wears more than one hat during the day, but in the church office, I need a rack with at least a half dozen buckhorns to hold all the hats I've accumulated while serving there. Here are a few titles on my bonnets:

Complaint Department: Every organization has one, and I've found our portal for complaints to be the first door that opens on Monday morning—the office. This hat has earflaps like the winter caps my grandfather wore when he did chores. My cap is beginning to look a bit frayed around the edges and is soiled from unconstructive criticism and one-sided suggestions. When I retire, I'll be tossing this hat into the circular filing bin alongside the complaints.

Floral Designer: I wear this lightweight cap when the altar flowers go unclaimed from Sunday's service. I delight in making little bouquets out of the funereal-looking sprays to give to shut-ins. I always save a few flowers for the office to remind me that there *is* life outside the church office.

Executive Administrative Assistant: A fancy name for a secretary to the senior pastor. This hat fits well, except on the days when it feels as if it were squeezing my brains, giving me a tension headache. On the days I wear it as if I'm in an Easter parade.

Thank you, Lord, for giving me so many different hats to wear,

Take My Hands

*I've put my life in your hands. You won't drop me,
you'll never let me down.* Psalm 31:5

Have I really put my life in God's hands? I'm good at seeking his love, guidance, comfort, and forgiveness, but I want the freedom of running my life *my* way. In the end, God must see me as a little kid holding on to one leg of her favorite doll while trying to pry it away from a friend, and saying, "Mine."

God must get weary from the way I cling to him one moment and then pull away from the grip of his hand. Hands connect one to another—they also show weakness and strength. I look at my hands and can see why I would never be chosen to model a ring or a new color of fingernail polish. I call them "farm-woman" hands, because they resemble those of my mother and grandmother, who worked hard on the farm. My knuckles bulge, the forefingers are crooked, veins protrude, and brown spots freckle the skin.

However, when I turn over my hands, the skin of the palms is smooth and soft. The lifelines are the same ones that were imprinted in my baby book. A palm reader might say I will have a long life, and that I am willing to share, and that I am a hard worker.

As I work on the computer, file papers, fix a jammed copy machine, or shake someone else's hands, I know that my hands are essential in my ministry in the church office. But they work best when I reach out and hold firmly on to one of God's hands.

*Lord, take my hands and let them move at the impulse
of Thy love* [Verse 2 from hymn: *Take My Life and Let It Be*
by Frances R. Havergal, 1874, Public Domain.]

Training Wheels

Since Jesus went through everything you're going through and more, learn to think like him. 1 Peter 4:1

I sometimes forget Jesus was human—he lived among sinners, and yet he remained sinless. He experienced heartache, grief, abuse, rejection, betrayal, and pain. As he carried the cross on the path to his own crucifixion, he knew his destiny. He could think like his Father because he was *of* his Father.

To think like Jesus means that I have to start thinking beyond my selfish ways. After the tornado went through Joplin, Missouri, I said to my husband, "For our vacation this summer we should pack up the motor home and go to Joplin to see how we can help." But within the next few days, I found myself searching the internet looking for a ticket to fly to New Jersey to celebrate our grandson Mason's first birthday. What would Jesus have done?

I have a job that keeps me tethered to my desk at the church most of the year. One day when having coffee with a friend, I said, "I don't feel as if I'm doing enough at church." She rattled off, "You write books for church secretaries, post a daily meditation blog, and lead retreats. Isn't that enough for now?"

I still want to go to Joplin, or other places that have experienced disasters, but for now, I believe God is telling me to think in real time: "Linda, family is important, too. Find another way to help people in your own neighborhood until you can go out and help others farther away."

Lord, thank you for reminding me that if I think like Jesus,
I'll find the answers to everyday problems and concerns,

Oh, the Places You Will Go!

*Your life is a journey you must travel with a deep
consciousness of God.* 1 Peter 1:18

I gave a friend a copy of *Oh, the Places You Will Go* by Dr. Seuss when she was terminated from the job that she dearly loved. The book tells about opportunities of discovery when starting out on a new journey. But there are places you don't want to go!

According to a forwarded e-mail I recently received, the writer has never been in Cahoots, because you can't go there alone. She's never been in Cognito. After all, who wants to go somewhere you'd never be recognized? She did claim to have been in Sane a few times, thanks to her family, friends, and co-workers who drove her there.

She's working out with the track team, practicing how to jump to Conclusions. I've heard she's been in Doubt a few times—a place to go when trust in someone or something has been shattered. I think she might be in Flexible, but she insists she's in Capable to move at all the older she gets.

A fun place to send the writer next year on vacation is a place called in(n) Suspense. The stimuli could be good for her heart. Even then, she will insist she's in Vincible and will resist leaving her office (in fear someone will discover she is not).

If I suggest to her that she is in Denial, she'll just say that she has never been there and is never going out of fear of landing in Deep Doodoo.

Oh, the places we go whether we want to or not.

*Dear Lord, help us land in places that give
us a spiritual boost each day,*

Expectations

I'm not saying that I have this all together, that I have it made.
But I am well on my way, reaching out for Christ, who has
so wondrously reached out for me. Philippians 3:12

"Jack of all trades, master of none" is how I describe myself, and those who know me well will say I'm certainly not a "Johnny do-it-all." [A phrase from a 1592 booklet, *Greene's Groats-Worth of Wit.*] "However, I've got my eye on the goal, where God is beckoning us onward—to Jesus. I'm off and running, and I'm not turning back." [Philippians 3:13,14]

I'm a firm believer in discovering what people expect of me and feel it is important to let them know my expectations for them. In the workplace, no job description is thorough enough to define expectations with respect to working relationships.

After beginning a new job, it takes time to figure what makes everyone "tick," let alone trying to figure out what is expected of the new employee. I've worked in my position for nearly three years, and each week at least one occasion arises in which I ask a question, such as, "Whose job is it to let the maintenance man know he needs to vacuum the crumbs beneath the boardroom table?"

Common sense helps us read between the lines of the job description. But unfortunately, God doesn't gift everyone with the ability to come up with sound and prudent judgments all the time. That's when I draw upon a communication skill I learned as a child: "From my little blue eyes I see crumbs on the floor in the boardroom" and just hope the hint gets picked up by the right set of ears or eyes.

Dear Lord, help us to communicate expectations
and graciously receive them in return,

Time War

There's an opportune time to do things, a right time
for everything on the earth. Ecclesiastes 3:1

Sculptor and poet Henry Van Dyke said, "Time is too slow for those who wait, too swift for those who fear, too long for those who grieve, too short for those who rejoice, but for those who love—time is eternity."

Do you have a big clock in your office, another in the copy room, a watch on your wrist? During a busy day, do you even have time to glance at a clock? Or, do you watch the minutes tick away waiting for the day to end?

Time is our friend and/or our enemy—well summed up by Van Dyke. If you tell a child to sit for an hour and read a book, it might seem as if you've given her or him a life sentence (unless the child loves to read). For me to take an hour to sit and read isn't a luxury, it's a necessity. My day goes better if I spend the first hour with God, my books, Bible, and journal.

When I'm working, I have little control over incidents that chew up my time. Recently I missed a 2:00 p.m. appointment with my hairdresser. I thought about it earlier in the day, but at 1:30 a member of the church came to my office and needed copies for a meeting that afternoon. Then the telephone rang. You guessed it, I forgot about my haircut. My hairdresser was not happy with me. I rescheduled and missed the next one! By then my hairdresser said, "Linda, I turned away another client for your appointment. I will have to charge you for your missed appointment." I agreed. I paid her and left still needing a haircut.

For another week, every time I looked in the mirror, it reminded me how much I needed to get control of the hours and minutes in my day.

Lord, you are the giver of time. Let me use it to your glory,

Retiring, Again

"Smoke, nothing but smoke . . . There's nothing to anythin,
all smoke. What's there to show for a lifetime of work, a ,
of working your fingers to the bone? Ecclesiastes 1:1

On April 15, 2012, I retired, again. The first two retirements were only practice to learn how to *really* retire. Working in the church is like a magnet to my soul. When I work, I feel better about myself. I like patterns in my day—getting dressed and out the door to make it to the office by 8:00 a.m. I like the associations I have with the people at the church, but mostly, I like being needed.

I must admit that I am only retiring from a paid job. My ministry will continue as I write books and stories (pitched to *Guideposts* and *Angels on Earth* magazines) and traveling around the United States having lunch with church staff to gather stories for my next book.

So what's at the end of my life? According to the author of Ecclesiastes (David's son), my life is nothing but smoke. If you've ever watched a campfire, you know that smoke is there one minute and gone as soon as the campfire is doused with water. My passion for writing is deep in my soul, and even when editors pass on a story or publishers don't see the value of a book I've written, they can't pour enough water on my soul to make me retire from serving God through the written and spoken word.

May you know when it is time to retire, and may you find blessings for the rest of your life—not just smoke.

Dear Lord, you give us opportunities. Let us face the
future knowing that you are there to lead us,

Open Mouth, Insert Foot

Don't shoot off your mouth, or speak before you think.
Don't be too quick to tell God what you think he wants to hear.
God's in charge, not you—the less you speak, the better.
Ecclesiastes 5:2

"Life is easily compared to a donut, There is too
many sides to bite at a time and it is always
going to leave you empty inside."—unknown

Maybe it's because I'm a writer and speaker, I tend to be a bit flippant, and I recognize that I can also be sarcastic or cynical. Sometimes words spew out of my mouth as if I've turned on the water tap, and instead of the careless words falling on ears, I wish they had gone down the drain.

My daughter was down on herself. She was overwhelmed with the responsibility of caring for foster children. While chatting, she said, "Maybe I'm too much of a micro-manager to be a mother." Without thinking, I said with a sarcastic twist, "You think?" Two little words affirmed her moment of frustration about parenting, and she said, "Mother, sometimes I just want you to listen." Ouch.

I had not meant to convey that my daughter wouldn't be a good mother. If I had taken time to frame my response, it would have come out like this: "I can see how frustrated you are, but being a good manager doesn't mean you can't also be a good mother." But it was too late to justify how I thought. The two evil words were all she heard.

God gave us two ears and one mouth for a good reason. We need to listen twice as hard to know how to respond to those we encounter. In some cases, there aren't any words that the speaker wants to hear from us, other than "I'm sorry."

Dear Lord, help me bridle the enthusiasm
I have to tell others what I think,

Strike Three! You're Out

I was hungry and you fed me, I was thirsty and you gave me a drink,
I was homeless and you gave me a room, I was shivering and
you gave me clothes, I was sick and you stopped to visit,
I was in prison and you came to me. Matthew 25:36

In today's scripture, Jesus had another teaching session with his disciples. He referred to people as sheep or goats—the sheep were the good guys and the goats, the bad guys. When he said the "sheep" had fed, clothed, and housed him, the disciples didn't understand, because they had never seen Jesus in a situation of being needy. He answered them, "Whenever you did one of these things to someone overlooked or ignored, that was me—you did it to me." (Matthew 25:40)

Three strikes and you're out—like in baseball. In reading today's scripture, I am reminded that I haven't opened my pantry often enough to share from my wealth of food (strike one). I have more coats in my closet than I need for Arizona's climate (strike two). But I do feel good about the spare bedroom in our home that has been occupied many times by teens and young adults who needed time to adjust to their current situation. No strikeout for now, but I can't think that I've hit a home run, either. There will always be someone who needs a safe place to land.

Lord, I get it. Today I'm opening my pantry and filling a
grocery bag for the food pantry, and I'm picking a coat from my
closet to give to a shelter. Thank you for the reminder.

According to SparkPeople.com's Fitness Tracker, a 150-pound
woman who walks briskly at a 15-minute mile pace (4 mph)
will burn 5 calories per minute. To burn off the donut
you'd have to walk around the office (at this quick pace) for
48 minutes, which is just over 3 miles! [Author comment:
Keep a pair of walking shoes under your desk.]

Don't Just Count Sheep

Overwork makes for restless sleep. Ecclesiastes 5:3

Some mornings I wake up thinking about the work I left on my desk the day before. That's unproductive time, because I don't get paid extra money to worry about the office after hours. Jessika Toothman from the TLC Website wrote *5 Tips for Leaving Work at the Office*. In a nutshell, they are:

1. **Learn when to say "no" and when to say "yes."** There are times we can't avoid taking work home or staying late to finish a project. Because there are no work detectives to check to see if it is necessary to forfeit your at-home time with company stuff, you need to police yourself.

2. **Find balance.** If the faster you work, the "behinder" you get, perhaps you need help with organization, or a discussion with your supervisor, to get help with the work you never get to.

3. **Wind down the workday.** Do a quick survey of what you didn't accomplish and move it into the flight pattern for the next day. Begin to think about what you want to do that evening at home with your family or friends.

4. **Transition into "me" time.** When you step foot into your house, you are on "me" time. Do something for yourself—something fun or good for your body—before even thinking about work again.

5. **Break the electronic chains.** When the cord was removed from the telephone, the phone became an extension of my arm. Although I would not like to go back to the days of a short cord, I have detached myself from the idea that I need to know everything all the time, which takes a lot of faith!

"Blessed is the person who is too busy to worry in the daytime and too sleepy to worry at night."—Source Unknown

Dear Lord, may I be busy at work and sleepy at night,

Laugh or Cry

*Crying is better than laughing. It blotches
the face but it scours the heart. Ecclesiastes 7:3*

As a little kid, when something upset me I'd cry. My father would call me "Crybaby," which only made me more upset. He grew up in a home with little affection, and I'm guessing tears weren't acceptable—especially to a man. But his mean comment worked: I'd shut off the tear valve and stuff my feelings deep into my gut.

When I was a teenager, I found an article in a *Reader's Digest* magazine titled "A Case for Crying," about how shedding tears can keep you sane. With this revelation, I decided it was no longer a sin to be a crybaby.

Babies and children cry until they learn to verbalize how they feel or what they need. As an adult, sometimes the only way I can communicate how I feel is to cry. However, I hate to cry in public. Not only do I end up with red eyes and blotches all over my face, I feel as if I've shown my vulnerability and sensitive nature—blowing my cover as someone always in control. The last good cry I remember happened at the office following a conflict with a co-worker. I had put up with enough criticism and complaints. Rather than blast the co-worker, I sat with the assistant pastor in her office crying like a baby.

The volume of tears I shed represented a reservoir of bad feelings, fears, frustrations, insecurity, and from being overworked and too tired. Like God, caring people see someone with a tear-stained face as a person doing a good job of housecleaning the heart.

Recently I found the tear-stained article about crying and pinned it on my bulletin board. It serves me as a reminder that tears are okay—even in public!

Dear Lord, remind me that I can cry on your shoulder any time,

Flying Off the Handle

Don't be quick to fly off the handle. Anger boomerangs.
You can spot a fool by the lumps on his head. Ecclesiastes 7:9

The Phrase Finder website says that "to fly off the handle" is an old American phrase alluding to the uncontrollable way a loose axe-head flies off its handle. A dangerous situation!

Redheads have often been stereotyped as being fiery-tempered. My husband's family has redheads, and according to his mother, the rest of the family dodged loose axe-heads on a regular basis. Perhaps a mutated gene causes someone to have both red hair and a hot temper!

Regardless of the color of hair, there is no room for anyone to fly off the handle in the office. I must admit that on one occasion I received a "lump on my head" from an encounter with a strong-willed paralegal. I was the office manager, and she had stepped on every one of my toes at least once during her tenure in the office. One day we took our disagreement outside the door of the office, and as we were in each other's face, we were caught by one of the attorneys. He cut our encounter short and insisted we take our problems to the conference room where it belonged.

Unfortunately, when tempers flare, there isn't a lot of rational thinking going on. "Shall we go to the conference room and yell at each other?"

It takes at least two people to have a conflict, but it takes only one person to bow out and not let the situation get worse.

Lord, I pray that the only lumps I get on my head
are from the ones I give myself when my temper flares,

The Good Old Days

Don't always be asking, "Where are the good old days?"
Wise folks don't ask questions like that. Ecclesiastes 7:10

This is Old Testament scripture! Can you imagine what the author would think about the "good old days" of the past century? We've gone through the luxury of having a few mechanical objects in the office to nearly everything being run by computer chips smaller than a fingernail.

Missing from the *good old days* are the standards and ethics taught to me by teachers, coaches, pastors, and my parents, such as the following lessons:

1. **Sports were a luxury.** When I played basketball in high school, the coach expected the players to keep their grades up, not to drink or smoke, and to play fairly. No one was exempt from these rules. If you screwed up, you hurt the whole team, not just yourself. The only exception to the rules was: *There are no exceptions to the rules!*

2. **Solid work ethic.** My parents taught me to work for spending money and to contribute to the family expenses. I babysat, cleaned houses, shoveled snow, and picked strawberries. My brothers had paper routes, worked in warehouses, and picked strawberries. We learned that a quarter is a quarter and how much a quarter could purchase. There were no credit cards.

3. **Honor authority.** No matter how much I disliked a teacher, I was not to bad-mouth her or him. Sometimes I liked some teachers better than others, but I always knew that if I passed the class, I could move on.

In the office, there aren't as many things from the "good old days" that I miss—especially mimeograph stencils, carbon paper, and my first really slow IBM computer (which I used to think was the best thing since sliced bread).

Lord, let us remember the past by honoring the present,

Good Days; Bad Days

On a good day, enjoy yourself; on a bad day, examine
your conscience. God arranges for both kinds of days
so that we won't take anything for granted. Ecclesiastes 7:14

I'm not so sure the author of Ecclesiastes (King David's son) ever had a bad day. Even if I were to work in total isolation, I could find ways to screw up a project or forget about an important deadline.

My top ten bad days at the office:
  10. A child got sick, and I was the only one around to clean up the mess;
   9. The family I found to help for Christmas defrauded other churches in the community, too;
   8. My boss confessed that he had been unfaithful to his wife;
   7. My favorite pastor/boss (not the same one that had an affair) announced his retirement;
   6. I backed into another car in the parking lot at a body repair shop after dropping a co-worker off to pick up her car;
   5. Someone stole my wallet from underneath my desk the week before Christmas;
   4. Cutbacks in the budget sent a couple of my co-workers out looking for new jobs;
   3. I failed to read the fine print on a contract that cost the office a lot of money;
   2. I ate a bad tuna salad sandwich and spent the rest of the day in the ladies' room; and
   1. Someone ate the last chocolate donut I'd been eyeing all morning.

My top good days: All the rest of the days!

Dear Lord, be with us through the bad and good days in the office,

Pssst—Can You Speak Louder?

Don't eavesdrop on the conversation of others.
What if the gossip is about you, and you'd rather not hear it?
You've done that a few times, haven't you—said things
behind someone's back you wouldn't say to his face?
Ecclesiastes 7:21,22

One of my least favorite shows on television is *TMZ*, in which the reporters look for uncompromising situations of famous people. Then the cast laughs and carries on as if it's the funniest thing on earth. This type of gossip (and that from the tabloid industry) serves for no good purpose other than making money.

Unfortunately, gossip isn't exclusive to *TMZ*. I must admit that it is confusing trying to discern what is really considered gossip. Paraphrased from an article by Gene Taylor (Centerville Road Church of Christ in Tallahassee, Florida), gossip occurs when:

➤ we share news or information about someone that does not compliment them—especially with an attitude of entertainment;

➤ we are looking to build ourselves up by tearing someone else down;

➤ we are trying to get even with someone;

➤ we don't like someone and get satisfaction out of sharing their failures or problems; and

➤ we talk about someone just to have something to say.

If these gossiping scenarios are taking place in your office, perhaps it's time to start a reality TV show: "The Gossip."

Dear God, help me curb my appetite for sharing
harmful information about people you love,

Office Traps

Take care of yourself, have a good time, and make the most of
whatever job you have for as long as God gives you life.
Ecclesiastes 7:20

Everyone who works in an office—secular or in the church—needs to be aware of traps that can affect the well-being and longevity of employees. The following are the most common pitfalls I've observed:

1. **Stress:** It lurks in every corner, underneath desks, hides in filing cabinets. Refresh yourself with breaks, give up grazing on food that robs your energy, and bind up stress with prayer.

2. **Balance:** A high-wire act in which you need to protect your time by setting boundaries, making to-do lists, and reviewing your job description from time to time to keep from a fatal fall.

3. **Communication:** Modern electronic communication aids don't replace the need for one-on-one conversations. It is important to find the mode of communication that is most effective for your staff.

4. **Expectations:** Job descriptions, manuals, guidelines, and personnel handbooks answer questions and solve disputes (when they are used!).

5. **Meetings:** To meet regularly on common ground with the whole staff helps to keep the ministry of the church moving forward.

6. **Praying:** A church staff that prays together stays together (or at least has a better chance of survival).

Dear God, please help our staff from
wandering into a danger zone,

Talking Ministry

You—I'm talking to all of you, everyone out here on the streets!
Proverbs 8:1

As she tidied up the reception desk, Mary, my Wednesday morning volunteer, said, "I'm sorry I couldn't have been more helpful today. All I did was answer the phone a few times." I answered Mary by saying: "For every time you answered the phone, I got closer to getting something done in my office."

What Mary missed in her self-evaluation is the gift of time she gave to everyone who walked into the office. Many members of our church stop by the office with a pretense of needing information or having forgotten to sign up for an event, but I know their secret: They want to talk to someone who will listen.

However, when a conversation begins to consume your time, you may need a few "tried and true" conversation stoppers:

- Look at your watch and say, "I'm enjoying our conversation, but I've got an appointment." (It may be with the copy machine or at the restroom.)
- Grab your jacket. "Let me walk you to the door. I'm on my way to my car to get something." (Surely, there is something you need in your car!)
- Glance at your calendar. "How about coming back next week and having coffee with me during my afternoon break?" (A real coffee break would be nice.)
- Mess with the papers on your desk. "I'd better get the bulletin ready for the copy volunteer, or I'll have to run it myself!" (That has happened!)

God, I pray that the lines of communication
will always be open with you,

Wind and Wings

Look at the birds, free and unfettered, not tied down to a job description, careless in the care of God. And you count far more to him than birds. Matthew 6:25

An eagle does three things every day. She sits on her roost, flaps her wings, and soars. Roosting or sitting on a branch is the safest activity. The perch provides both a place for rest and an observation post for hunting. Before she flaps her wings, either to hunt or to soar, she must let go of her steel-trap grip on the branch. Flapping her powerful wings is a sight to see! The action seems so effortless, yet it takes a great deal of energy and skill to lift her body well above the earth.

Soaring is what makes an eagle an eagle—gracefully moving in ever-widening circles. Yet, before she soars, she must do one thing: Stop flapping. The eagle can't flap and soar at the same time.

For many of us, when we began our call in the church office, it was similar to a baby eagle learning to fly on its own. It is said that a mother eagle pads the nest to make a soft place for her eggs to hatch and to begin life. As the babies grow, the mother eagle tosses the soft down out of the nest to make it less homey and comfortable. Then one day she begins to boot the babies out of the nest, but soars close by to catch a flailing baby before it falls to the ground. The mother eagle repeats this behavior until the young eagles realize they can fly on their own strength.

Where are you in your stage of development as part of the church staff? Some may be lounging in the nest on a comfy cushion; others may be wriggling around in the nest ready to move on to the next stage. Many are learning to fly, and some are soaring with the other eagles. It makes no difference where you are in your journey. We all need to depend on God for the wind beneath our wings.

Lord, give me strong wings and a good upward draft of wind,

Lighten the Load

We've been surrounded and battered by troubles,
but we're not demoralized; we're not sure what to do,
but we know that God knows what to do. 2 Corinthians 4:8

I read a meditation about the explorer Samuel Hearne who, while leading a group on a vigorous expedition in northern Canada, had most of the rations stolen by thieves. Hearne recorded in his journal: "The weight of our baggage being lightened, our next day's journey was more swift and pleasant."

That's what I call an "attitude of gratitude," or perhaps the high altitude made him giddy. Nevertheless, there are blessings in lightening any of our loads at the office.

Today, we rely on the power of the internet and mostly communicate by e-mail. I've heard of executives who have hundreds of new e-mails to pore through every day! I wonder if the senders of these e-mail messages would have bothered to convey their message if they had to print out a letter and envelope and get it to the mailbox.

E-mail is here to stay, until adventuresome computer programmers come up with something better—to lighten our load. Until then, there are ways to help keep your in-box from becoming a burden to your day:

1. Guard your e-mail address.
2. Use a spam filter.
3. Think carefully before hitting "reply to all."
4. Unsubscribe to unwanted e-mail.
5. Talk! Reach for the telephone on your desk, or stretch your legs by strolling up or down the hallway to speak to someone face to face. Maybe this will be the creative way we communicate in the twenty-second century!

Dear Lord, thank you for the ease of communicating with you—
no spam, no failed connections, and no rejections,

Embrace Mistakes

Every part of Scripture is God-breathed and useful one way or another—
showing us truth, exposing our rebellion, correcting our mistakes,
training us to live God's way. 2 Timothy 3:16

I may go down in the history books in my church as the secretary who made the most mistakes. Often I catch the mistakes of my co-workers before they become fodder for public scrutiny. However, the angel God sends to watch over me at the office doesn't proofread, and there is no "errors and omissions" department in our church.

Most of the members of the church are grace-filled and don't dwell on finding errors. However, there seems to be one self-appointed member in every church who serves to police everything that comes out of the office. Whenever I get the "policeman's" call or a written note left on my desk, I want to spew scripture from Ephesians 4:29: "Watch the way you talk . . . Say only what helps, each word is a gift."

The old saying, "Sticks and stones can break my bones, but words can never hurt me," is a bunch of baloney. Words hurt. Being wrong, or making a non-earth-shattering mistake, is an opportunity to learn a lesson. Ken Robinson, a British author, speaker, and international advisor once said, "If you're not prepared to be wrong, you'll never come up with anything original."

As a writer, I remember how the sight of red pencil marks on my manuscripts made me think I should quit writing. Now, I'm grateful for the editor who comes behind me and mops up my messes (and for word processing that makes it easy to make corrections).

Dear Lord, let me dwell in the house of forgiveness,

Discovering Gifts

God's various gifts are handed out everywhere;
but they all originate in God's Spirit. 1 Corinthians 12:4

A few years ago, I discovered the gift of writing during a time of personal turmoil. As part of a journaling class, I read aloud my deepest thoughts and concerns that I had just written. One of the participants said, "Your writing inspires me. Keep it up!"

After that comment, it was as if God gave me permission to open the gift he had wrapped and left under my Christmas tree for over sixty years. Before my crisis, I wouldn't have recognized (or gratefully received) the gift of writing and public speaking.

One question I am frequently asked after a presentation is, "How do you remember so many incidents to write about in your books?" That's easy to answer. "I don't," I tell them. "The Holy Spirit pokes around in my memory bank and pulls out one story at a time." When I begin to write a story or devotion and find that I'm laboring over words, sentences, and paragraphs, it's a sign to me that I'm not tuned in to my spiritual channel.

Every morning I welcome the new day in my screened-in porch, or when it's too chilly outside, I find a place to sit by a sunny window. While sipping on a cup of hot tea, I spend time alone with God—as much time as I need to pray and to read from a selection of devotional books and my Bible—The Message. Then I record my thoughts on my blog, "Daily Meditation Moment" (at http://souly4youbylindagillis.com).

For every minute I spend in this quiet manner, the Holy Spirit refills my drained spiritual pool—just enough to get me to the next morning.

Dear Lord, help me use my gifts from you to
encourage others to use their gifts,

Missionary in Training

The congregation in Antioch was blessed with a number of prophet-preachers and teachers . . . . One day as they were worshiping God . . . , the Holy Spirit spoke: "Take Barnabas and Saul and commission them for the work I have called them to do." Acts 13:1,2

Barnabas, one of the first Christian missionaries, had been empowered by the Holy Spirit to travel to virgin territory and break the news to everyone about Jesus.

The first time I heard a presentation by a missionary on assignment to Africa, I thought, *It would be great to be a missionary!* However, then the "buts" started . . . I couldn't live in a foreign country by myself . . . learn a tribal language . . . sleep on a mat in a hut made of mud . . . eat rice three times a day, and most certainly, I could never leave my family for years at a time.

We don't have to go outside our country's borders to be a missionary. The Center for United States Missions says that the U.S. is one of the top three mission fields in the world! At a large church where I once worked, everyone knew the mission statement: *Making Jesus Known.* Every Sunday as the service ended, the pastor said, "Go in peace; serve the world"—the world that began where the sidewalk met the pavement in the parking lot.

God knows my heart and would not call me to serve outside of my comfort zone. But by working in the church office, I feel called into ministry and mission, starting at my desk.

Dear Savior, let me learn more about
you by telling your stories to others,

Motto printed on each box of donuts sold
in Levitt's Mayflower coffee and donut shops:
"As you ramble on through life, brother, whatever be your
goal, keep your eye upon the donut and not upon the hole."

Chewing Gum

f you forgive sins, they're gone for good. If you don't forgive sins,
what are you going to do with them? John 20:23

Forgiving someone who has sinned against me is hard—just plain hard. I'd rather chew on that sinful act like a piece of gum until the flavor is gone and then pop another "stick of gum" into my mouth to get another burst of the flavor of anger and hurt.

In the above scripture, Jesus asks a good question: What are you going to do with the unforgiven sins? Scientists believe that stress causes the body to break down. Nothing is more stressful than carrying around a backpack of unforgiven sins!

Sometimes, before either side of a conflict can give or receive forgiveness, there needs to be time to work through the what's, why's, and how's that caused the situation. Without clarity, resentment is added to the overstressed backpack.

Recently, I felt abandoned at an airport when a friend failed to pick me up for a scheduled overnight visit. For days I mulled the incident in my mind—I could understand how schedules are mixed up, but when she didn't offer a solution for the problem, I was hurt . . . perhaps we could have met for coffee. I wrote her an e-mail and said, "I'm so disappointed I didn't get to see you last week." Her response came with an explanation, and an apology. In return, my response was simply, "I love you."

God provides the path for forgiveness by breathing the Holy Spirit on us. The time and way to forgive will be revealed through prayer and meditating on God's Word. I have found that it is not any easier to forgive myself than to forgive others. It is humbling to admit that perhaps I was part of the problem and then have to look someone in the eye and ask, "Will you forgive me?"

Lord, I am grateful for the peace I receive
when I forgive those who sin against me,

Pick a Day

On the seventh day, he rested from all work . . .
and made it a Holy Day. Genesis 2:2

Nowhere in the Bible does it say that Sunday was named as the Holy Day. I'm not a biblical scholar, nor a history buff, so I don't know how Sunday became the "Seventh Day." (Perhaps I'll Google for the information when I find the time.)

Calendars usually feature Sunday as the first day of the week. Perhaps it's indicating that everyone should rest before going back to work on Monday. It's common on Monday morning to hear, "I can't wait until next weekend." To rest? Not likely. Those who fill their weekends with too much work (or play), go back to work on Monday more tired than when they left on Friday.

While growing up in a conservative Norwegian family, Sunday was *the* day of rest. At Grandma's house, I couldn't dance or play cards on Sunday. We took naps, read books, visited relatives or friends.

Today, it's not easy to set aside Sunday as a day of rest. Folks work long hours during the week, and weekends turn into time to catch up on errands and household chores. Kids are encouraged to participate in sports, which often occur on Sundays. The newspapers are full of advertisements that lure us out to shop.

Even though Sunday remains the most common day to go to church, one can pick any day of the week to kick back, rest, and spend time with God. If a full day is impossible to set aside, try sabbatical moments to pull away from the busy world for a few minutes to meditate on everything you are missing by being too busy.

Dear Lord, you gave us permission to take a day of rest.
Help us to give ourselves permission to do so,

Bind Us Together, Lord

Abraham was a hundred years old when his son Isaac was born. Sarah said, God has blessed me with laughter and all who get the news will laugh with me! Genesis 21:5

"Your sense of humor is one of the most powerful tools you have to make certain that your daily mood and emotional state support good health." —Paul E. McGhee, Ph.D.

I have had bad hair days, days with wardrobe malfunctions (not like the ones exploited on You Tube), and on one occasion, a day of wearing a navy blue shoe and a black shoe to the office. I didn't notice the mismatched shoes until taking a break around noon. For the rest of the day I laughed at myself every time I looked down at my feet. I even pointed out my crazy-shoe day to others, and they laughed, too.

Laughter is good for the soul, and is especially helpful when working in an office. When we laugh at one another's humorous situations, it reminds us that we are humans working in a divine setting. Unlike contaminating the office by coughing or sneezing, laughter is a good infection. It's been said that laughter can strengthen the immune system, increase one's energy level, and help one to forget about a pain in the back or neck! All this without popping another pill into the mouth. On the social level, laughter binds people together, eases conflict, and lightens burdens.

Every month a group of six to eight volunteers collate, label, and sort the newsletter to be bulk-mailed. From my office, I can hear them laughing. The joyful sound makes me want to join them—just to get in on some of that free medicine.

Dear Lord, you gave us the gift of laughter;
help us remember to use it freely,

If the Shoe Fits

If I were in your shoes, I'd go straight to God, I'd throw myself on the mercy of God. Job 5:8

In researching the words "sole and soul" in regard to the name of my website (www.souly4you by LindaGillis.com), I came up with a few comparisons about shoes (defined by the heel) and the souls of those who walk into the church office.

Pump: The classic, most popular high heel *or* the person who hangs around your desk trying to get information about someone else.

Stiletto: A thin, pointy, and high heel *or* anyone who thinks they can do nothing wrong.

Wedge: A heel that forms a triangle *or* a person who tries to put you in between two other people in a conflict situation.

Chunky: A sturdy heel—high or low *or* the one who gets behind your back and protects you.

Platform: A shoe with a thick sole under the front portion of the foot *or* the person (or people) who stirs up trouble by thinking it's their way or no way at all.

Clog: The heel is the same level from front to back *or* like the person who can't make up his or her mind.

Sling back: A strap wraps around the back of the exposed foot *or* a person who shows up when you begin to fall.

Sandals: The majority of the foot is exposed—like the souls of most people in the church. You know the old saying, "If the shoe fits, wear it."

Lord, let me wear the type of shoes that help me serve you in the church office,

Staffing Needs

*He climbed a mountain and invited those he wanted with him . . . He
settled on twelve, and designated them apostles.* Matthew 10:13

Should you be involved in the process of hiring new office support
staff? Staff turnover is often the best opportunity for a church to
re-evaluate their administrative needs. No one knows more about
what an office needs than a veteran office employee. Unless a pastor
or chairman of the personnel committee has actually been a church
secretary, they have little understanding of the dynamics of working
in a church office—the interruptions, expectations of the members,
dealing with multiple bosses, etc.

Consider the following questions when re-staffing an office:
- Has the size of the congregation and/or staff changed since
  the last employee was hired?
- What level of competency and experience is needed to make
  the office run efficiently?
- Without consideration of the budget for staff salaries and
  benefits, how many total hours are needed to handle the
  expected and unexpected tasks of the church office?
- Is there room for adjustment to the current budget to find the
  best candidate for the office?
- Do you trust that God will provide a candidate who will see
  the position as ministry—different from the standards found
  in a secular office?
- Is there a possibility for a "job-share" position to help keep
  the office covered at all times?
- Is there someone on staff who has been moved from desk
  to desk? Jesus did well when he handpicked his disciples, but
  after all, he is God.

*Dear Lord, give good discerning skills to those
in charge of staffing the church office,*

Flickering

If you only look at us, you might well miss the brightness.
2 Corinthians 4:7,8

"This little light of mine, I'm going to let it shine . . .", but it may flicker and need to be relit. I'm just God's servant working in the body of a human being—flawed and full of mistakes . . . and failures. Some days I wonder why I choose to work in an environment with so many perfect people surrounding me!

One morning the first thing I heard was: "Who did the new member packets? They were a mess." I answered, "My volunteer." Then I learned how "you can't trust the volunteer" and "I always did them myself." Actually, my volunteer and I worked together to make the packets. An old copy of the constitution got in by mistake, a form was printed upside down, and there were some omissions. I should have double-checked the packets, but there simply wasn't time in my schedule.

In spite of my outside appearance (confident and in control), I have a sensitive side. When I fail to live up to someone else's expectations, I feel as if a neon sign is flashing on my forehead: **Incompetent.** So, when my co-worker brought up the packet problem, all I heard in my mind was, "The meeting was a failure because of you."

Being sensitive is a great quality for anyone who works in the church. Unfortunately, not everyone is equally sensitive and doesn't realize how hurtful it is when they "lay it on the line." My soft side needs to be stroked, like this: [With a smile in the voice] "You did a great job, Linda, getting the information ready for the new-member orientation. I can see you put a lot of work into it. Thank you so much! Sometime before the next new-member orientation, let's go over the material in the packets.

Lord, help us grow thick skin when we
have to face our human flaws,

Serving Hats

"Deeply moved, Jesus put out his hand, touched him." Mark 1:41

"May I be the one with 'Welcome' written on my smile
and 'Hello' etched upon my outstretched hand: The hand I
extend to every human who blesses me with presence."
— Joyce Rupp, O.S.M.

I've personalized the quote above to remind me that my job as a church secretary is to welcome and assist those who walk into the office. It's easy for me to want to dwell only on the projects I enjoy, such as preparing the newsletter and writing publicity notices. On the other hand, interruptions are my least favorite part of being a solo church secretary.

I wear many hats in the office. These are a few of them:

- **Hard Hat:** For the construction zone. Stay clear of my desk when its annual-report time!
- **Cowboy Hat:** In the kitchen shoveling out the mess left from the chili dinner.
- **Referee's Cap:** Needed for confrontation between the chairperson of the ladies' society and the janitor.
- **Sombrero:** Wake me when I'm finished proofing the bulletin.
- **Cap with Earmuffs:** Too many bosses with too much information coming to me from every angle.
- **Private Eye Hat:** On the search for my favorite pen.
- **Swim Cap:** Don when drowning in too much work . . . or self-pity.

Jesus might add one more hat to my collection—a crown embedded with the word LOVE.

Lord, help me pick the right hat at the right time to serve you,

Twins: Guilt and Grace

I'm absolutely convinced that nothing—nothing living or dead, angelic, or demonic, today or tomorrow, high or low, thinkable or unthinkable—absolutely nothing can get between us and God's love because of the way that Jesus our Master has embraced us.
Romans 8:34

Guilt: "A feeling that one is to blame for something."
Grace: "God's loving mercy toward mankind."
(*Oxford American Dictionary*)

Somehow, the word "guilt" ends up floating on top of my Alphabet Soup more often than I'd like. I am certain God uses guilt to nudge me when I open my personal e-mail at the office or have to recycle a stack of documents printed upside down.

Guilt is a solo journey in which one packs his or her own bag. Here are a few questions to ask yourself to find out if guilt is worth the cost of the trip:

- Are you judging yourself too harshly?
- Is someone getting your bag out of the closet?
- Do you see a good reason for the guilt you are dragging around with you? (Have you offended, used, abused, or ignored someone?)
- Are you hanging around someone who is constantly leading you down the wrong path?
- Do you find yourself taking the same dead-end guilt road because it has become a habit?

No matter how hard we try to live a sinless life, we will fail. We can thank guilt for being a friend and be even more grateful for its twin, grace.

Dear Lord, may I live a healthy balance between guilt and grace,

Haste Makes Waste

Ignorant zeal is worthless; haste makes waste. Proverbs 19:2

After being out of the church office for almost ten years, my first Christmas as a reinstated church secretary proved that I had forgotten how I needed all my mental faculties to do my job during busy seasons. So why did I invite all my kids to come home for the holidays?

It was tough having a houseful (eight extra to bed down and feed) and working while everyone at home was playing. On Christmas Eve Day, I still needed to go back to the church and collate the bulletins because my Friday volunteer was home enjoying her family. I brought my daughter, Susan, to the office to help me collate the bulletin. I figured we'd work fast, get it done in about an hour, and then we could finish our grocery shopping.

Susan started collating and then I heard her say, "Mom, there is something wrong with the bulletin." After looking at the pages, I tossed the whole mess in the recycling bin and had visions of leaving the office—for good! The day before, I had given the volunteer, who copies the bulletin, the draft as it had been printed out by the pastor (who also produced it), without looking over the project. Our normal Sunday bulletins are one page back-to-back. This one needed to be cut and pasted up as a booklet.

I sent Susan home. Frustrated (not close to how I really felt), I began the wait for the 300 copies of the colored cover to come off the printer. Four hours later, I locked up the office and went home.

The old saying, "Haste makes waste,"(from a book that belonged to Mary Bacon, a farmer's wife, in 1762), certainly applied to the hundreds of sheets of paper and the ink that it took to redo the bulletin that Christmas Eve.

Dear God, it humbles me when I make a mistake, but it refreshes me to relive the humble story of Jesus' birth every Christmas,

A New Year's Prayer

God spoke: "Lights! Come out! Shine in Heaven's sky! Separate Day from Night. Mark seasons and days and years . . ." Genesis 1:14

A new year—a new me. Not likely. I can't toss off my old ways and take on new ones by simply making a resolution. However, I do believe resolutions can be a powerful tool to help set goals for the next year. The trick is to align expectations with reality, considering what is realistic or not.

A new year's resolution for the church office needs to be completed by the first Sunday in Advent (a date established by counting backwards four Sundays from Christmas). Unlike the blank new Gregorian calendar I hang on my wall by January 1, the church calendar repeats itself and is full of regular holidays and events. During the year the unexpected events, such as marriages, funerals, baptisms, etc., fill in the days of the calendar and make for a busy office.

Let us begin the church year with this prayer:

Dear Lord, please give me . . .
A few friends who understand me and
remain my friends;
work to do which has real value,
without which the world would be the poorer;
a mind unafraid to travel, even though the trail
may not be blazed;
an understanding heart;
a sense of humor;
time for quiet, silent meditation;
a feeling of the presence of God;
the patience to wait for the coming of these things,
with the wisdom to recognize them when they come. Amen.
—Anonymous

Last word of
"The Donut Theory"

A Jelly Donut is a yummy mid-afternoon energy boost.
Two Jelly Donuts are an indulgent breakfast.
Three Jelly Donuts may induce a tummy ache.
Six Jelly Donuts—that's an eating disorder.
Twelve Jelly Donuts is fraternity pledge hazing.
My point is that you can have too much of a good thing
and overdoses are destructive.

—*David* Einhorn, President, Greenlight Capital, Inc.

Made in the USA
Lexington, KY
12 February 2014